ABOUT THE AUTHOR

MICHIO KAKU is a professor of theoretical physics at the City University of New York, cofounder of string field theory, and the author of several widely acclaimed science books and best sellers, including *Beyond Einstein, The Future of Humanity, The Future of the Mind, Hyperspace, Physics of the Future,* and *Physics of the Impossible.* He is the science correspondent for *CBS This Morning,* the host of the radio programs *Science Fantastic* and *Exploration,* and a host of several science TV specials for the BBC and the Discovery and Science Channels.

INTERNATIONAL SERIES OF MONOGRAPHS IN
EXPERIMENTAL PSYCHOLOGY

GENERAL EDITOR: H. J. EYSENCK

VOLUME 19

PSYCHIATRIC DIAGNOSIS:
A REVIEW OF RESEARCH

OTHER TITLES IN THE SERIES IN EXPERIMENTAL PSYCHOLOGY

PSYCHIATRIC DIAGNOSIS: A REVIEW OF RESEARCH

GEORGE FRANK

New York University

PERGAMON PRESS

Oxford · New York · Toronto · Sydney · Braunschweig

Pergamon Press Ltd., Headington Hill Hall, Oxford

Pergamon Press Inc., Maxwell House, Fairview Park, Elmsford,
New York 10523

Pergamon of Canada Ltd., 207 Queen's Quay West, Toronto 1

Pergamon Press (Aust.) Pty. Ltd., 19a Boundary Street,
Rushcutters Bay, N.S.W. 2011, Australia

Pergamon Press GmbH, Burgplatz 1, Braunschweig 3300, West Germany

First edition 1975

Library of Congress Cataloging in Publication Data

Frank George.
Psychiatric diagnosis: a review of research.

(International series of monographs in experimental psychology, v. 19)
Bibliography: p.
1. Mental illness.—Diagnosis. I. Title.
[DNLM: 1. Mental disorders–Diagnosis. W1 IN835K v. 19/WM141 F828p]
RC469.F7 1975   616.8'9'075   74-13884
ISBN 0-08-017712-3

Printed in Great Britain by A. Wheaton & Co., Exeter

CONTENTS

PROLOGUE

THIS is a study of the heuristic value of psychiatric diagnoses. As clinicians dealing with the psychological ills of man, we are ofttimes called upon to make a diagnosis. Presumably this is for a purpose: that is, the diagnosis should enable clinicians to make certain judgments regarding the life of the individual being diagnosed, else why diagnose? To make decisions, however, implies something upon which that judgment is made, be it faith, hope, wish, fantasy, or fact. When one has the responsibility of the welfare of other human beings, it behoves one to function more on fact than faith. If we are going to do more than play the taxonomic game—i.e., to name for the sake of naming—making a diagnosis should be tantamount to a shorthand way of saying certain things about the patient, e.g., where he is, psychologically, where he may be heading, psychologically, and perhaps something about the development of his problems, i.e., where he has been, psychologically. The big question, therefore, is whether a diagnosis affords us that kind of information. This, then, is the purpose of this research, viz., to determine what information *is* provided by a diagnostic statement re psychopathology.

To answer this question, I could have designed a study, but I chose not to. Many individuals have already designed many studies in this area. I reasoned, thus, that rather than conduct yet another study, why not profit from what my colleagues have done? Why not try to find the answer to the question posed above in the research that had already been done? This is what I hope to accomplish in this monograph.

Before I proceed with the presentation of the data, I wish to beg the reader's indulgence whilst I make three brief comments. First, as regards the degree of coverage: I have tried to cover as much of the research literature as I could find. However, as anyone knows who has ever attempted to write such a survey work, it is inevitable that the work of some authors gets omitted. Therefore, my first comment is a most sincere apology to anyone whose work has been left out of the review of studies; it was unintentional. My second comment takes the form of both an apology and a word of appreciation to my family, who have tolerated the vast amount of time out of the main stream of family life that writing this monograph has consumed. My third and final comment is a note of appreciation to the editors of Pergamon Press who have been so patient with me as I have struggled with this manuscript. In that category goes especial thanks to Professor Eysenck, General Editor of the International Series of Monographs in Experimental Psychology, for the honor he bestowed on me by inviting me to write this book for his Series, and for the encouragement and comments he afforded me along the way.

GEORGE FRANK

CHAPTER 1

THE DIAGNOSTIC PRINCIPLE

BEFORE we proceed with the analysis of the studies *per se*, we should confront the entire issue of why we diagnose in the first place. As regards the study of psychopathology, the need for a diagnosis seems to derive from our roots in science on the one hand and in medicine, the original clinical arm of science, on the other. From science we learn that one way to make meaning out of our data is to put it into some form, some order, some organization. In this way certain characteristics of the phenomena being studied become apparent, from which certain defining principles may emerge.

As Stagner has written:

> "Much of science consists of a search for adequate definitions. This is necessary not merely because man is generally happier when he has a neat system for classifying ideas; increasing precision of definitions frequently results in focusing research more sharply and revealing important truths which had previously been ignored" (Stagner, 1948, p. 1).

In medicine a diagnosis implies a defining of a process, which, in turn, implies some etiological factor, and, in turn, a possible course of therapeutic intervention. There are thus two very strong pulls on the clinician studying psychopathology to organize and, hence, categorize his data, both from scientific and practical considerations.

In science there are several modes of organizing data, the difference depending upon the nature of the data and the purpose for the classification. For example, there are purely descriptive systems of classification, based on parameters which only describe the structural aspects of phenomena, e.g., a tree is a large, fibrous plant, etc., a rock is a hard substance composed of . . . etc. However, the classification of phenomena that possess the capacity for extrinsic action (i.e., other than growing or decomposing over time, which I define as intrinsic action)

1

must take into account this additional dimension, viz., the functional properties of the elements. So it is with the human. To be meaningful, the classification of the data in psychiatry, i.e., of psychopathology, should not just *describe* the events, viz., the behavior, but provide other information as well. Since behavior (even that which we classify as psychopathological) is embedded in the matrix of an on-going life, the behavioral moment has a past, a present, and a future. A classification system of human behavior must relate to *all* of these dimensions if possible; that is there must be a statement about past, present, and future activity states. This is, as one might say, a tall order.

As regards psychopathology, many systems of classification have been offered over the years. By virtue of the fact that each system begets a revision, it seems safe to assume that none of the systems yet proferred have proven to be adequate. For purposes of our present study, we will utilize the current system of classification in psychiatry, that which was developed in 1968 (American Psychiatric Association, 1968). However, it should be of interest to the serious student of psychopathology to note the nature of the changes in these systems of classification over the years. This should provide us with the genetic context of the current system.

Temkin (1965) has observed that this history of the classification of psychopathology stretches back to the earliest records of scientific data. Reviews of the many systems of classification in psychiatry have been done by, for example, Franz Alexander (Alexander and Selesnick, 1966), Karl Menninger (Menninger, Mayman and Pruyser, 1963), Gregory Zilboorg (Zilboorg and Henry, 1941), as well as Lord and Fleming (1932), Parkin (1966a, b), Stainbrook (1953), Vieth (1957), Temkin (1965) and Watson (1949). Lord and Fleming observed the development of *nineteen* different systems of classification just from 1845 to 1932. Since 1931, history records at least five major revisions of the diagnostic schema (i.e., 1931, 1949, 1952, 1963 and 1968). In my estimation, Menninger *et al.* (1963) provide us with the most extensive review of the systems of classification of psychiatric phenomena I have come across. They note that at least as far back as 1400 B.C. a classification of psychiatric disorders existed in India which divided mental disorders into seven categories (though these categories are not described or defined in the book). Interestingly, when we get to Hippocrates, some

1000 years later, we find six categories [viz., phrenitis (acute mental disturbance with fever), mania (acute mental disturbance without fever), melancholia, epilepsy, hysteria, and "Scythian disease", i.e., transvestitism]. In terms of our current problems and efforts at classification, one notes that attempt of even the earliest formulations to try to differentiate disturbances due to some organic process and those not [thus Plato differentiated madness due to divine intervention (categorizing the various forms of disorder by the name of a god, e.g., prophetic madness induced by Apollo, religious madness induced by Dionysus, poetic madness induced by the Muses, and erotic madness induced by Aphrodite and Eros) and madness due to organic factors (which he called "natural madness")]. The classification systems offered by Hippocrates and Plato (around the fifth century B.C.) reflect attempts to struggle with aspects of behavior with which we still struggle, i.e., the attempt to go beyond mere description and to include, in the instance of their systems, etiological considerations as well. In this history of the systems of classification of psychopathology, a most interesting system was presented us by Immanuel Kant in 1798 (Kant, 1964). In this system, psychopathology was divided into disorders of mood or cognition. The classification of psychological disturbance presented by Kant was: amentia (what he referred to as "senselessness"), dementia (madness characterized by disturbance in logical thinking), insanity (absurd judgment), and frenzy (disorder of reason). One can see here the roots of some of the work that will follow a century later, as, for example, in the work of Kraeplin.

As, metaphorically, all roads lead to Rome, so do all "roads" in psychiatry seem to lead (back) to the work of Kraeplin. So important is his system of classification to an understanding of even the most current system of classification in psychiatry, that we should dwell on his ideas at some length. It is interesting to note that rather than being so unique, as those examinations of his ideas which do not view the total scene historically indicate, Kraeplin stands in meaningful relationship with that which went before. For example, we note that Kraeplin viewed insanity as being divided into those dealing with disorders of mood and those of cognition (as did, for example, Kant). Moreover, German psychiatry immediately prior to Kraeplin (e.g., Kahlbaum) attempted to make what were considered to be completely separate entities (e.g., paranoia, hebephrenia, depression, etc.) into larger, more comprehensive classes (e.g., disorders occurring at various stages of life, e.g., postnatally, during early development, after puberty, older age, and disorders of the nervous system, the vegetative system, and that having to do with sexuality). Furthermore, in the nineteenth century (hence, prior to Kraeplin), Morel began to classify according to etiology and outcome. Kraeplin, thus, becomes but a point in the development of the conceptual schema in psychiatry. Kraeplin's attempt to differentiate the disorders into various subgroups, the movement away from seeing disorders in isolation, but, rather, trying to relate some kinds of disorders with others, i.e., those where there seemed to be a meaningful link, and the attempt to integrate etiological and prognostic considerations into the descriptive, were the directions in which psychiatry had been moving in Germany and France just prior to Kraeplin. Kraeplin stands out, as we can now see, primarily because of the amalgam of these different intents in psychiatry into one system. If nothing else, Kraeplin's system can be seen in a matrix of thinking within psychiatry, and, if nothing else, places his thinking in its proper perspective. The great classifier presents us with a system with eight major categories (Kraeplin, 1902), placing the various aspects of psychological difficulties viz., disorders of perception, disorders of thinking, disturbances of judgment and reasoning, disturbances of the emotions, and disturbances of action and volitional behavior into the categories of: insanity due to external sources (acute, transitory disturbance due to infections, intoxication, or exhaustion), dementias, organic dementias (due to syphillitic infection, old age, metabolic or neurological disorders, epilepsy), emotional disorders (melancholia and manic-depressive psychoses), senility, psychogenic neuroses (hysterical insanity, traumatic neurosis, dread neurosis), psychopathy, and disorders due to defective intellectual development. One can see that the force of Kraeplin's ideas in psychiatry is ubiquitous.

Following Kraeplin, the list of categories expands, and the classification system which was used in psychiatry from World War I to World War II contained *twenty-four* categories: psychoses due to diseases, addictions, trauma, organic disorders, central nervous system deterioration, involutional psychoses, manic-depressive psychoses, dementia praecox, psychoses with psychopathic behavior, psychoses with mental deficiency, paranoid conditions, and the psychoneuroses.

The 1952 version of the official American Psychiatric Association's system of classification (American Psychiatric Association, 1952) had almost 100 specific diagnostic entities subsumed under seven large categories of behavior, viz., brain disorder, mental deficiency, psychogenic psychotic disorders, psychoneurotic disorders, personality disorders, and transient situational personality disorders. The 1968 version of the official APA system of classification (American Psychiatric Association, 1968) subsumed over 100 specific diagnostic entities under ten larger categories, including mental retardation, organic brain syndromes, psychophysiological disorders, transient situational disturbances, behavior disorders of childhood and of adolescence.

Spitzer and Wilson (1968) have analyzed the differences between the 1952 and 1968 versions. Amongst the differences they note:

(a) The names of some of the disorders are modified.
(b) There is a general elimination of the term "reaction", thereby seeming to abrogate the conceptual modification made by Meyer, in favor of a return to the more Kraeplinian typology.
(c) The 1952 system has seven major categories, the 1968 ten.
(d) Involutional psychotic reaction has been moved to (i.e., now included with) the section on major affective disorders, while psychotic depressive reaction is now a separate category.
(e) Changes have been made in the definition of several of the disorders.
(f) Recording of multiple psychiatric diagnoses is encouraged.

Yet despite the many revisions, as Shakow (1965) has noted, we have never seemed to find a truly satisfactory system of classification of psychopathology. The question remains as to whether the 1968 revision is any more meaningful than the previous ones. However, as we read through the various systems over the ages, we note an ever-increasing complexity; whether this complexity has led to any refinement in knowledge will be, in part, assessed by the analysis of these studies.

Cohen (1943) noted that diagnoses should be considered as shorthand statements to communicate information, and W. A. Hunt and his associates have written:

"Diagnosis is essentially the old familiar scientific process of classification, of introducing order into one's observations with an attendant increase in meaningfulness . . . It is the labeling of an object or phenomenon in order to indicate its inclusion in a class of similar objects . . . By placing the object in a certain class, it is possible to infer on the basis of this class membership possession of certain class characteristics by the object without the necessity of further experience of it. Diagnoses are carriers of information . . . They should be evaluated in terms of the economy with which they transmit information, the extent and accuracy of the information transmitted, and the functional importance or relevance of this information . . ." (Caverny *et al.*, 1955, p. 368).

Such an evaluation is exactly what we are about to attempt.

CHAPTER 2

THE METHODS

BY and large, psychiatry utilizes the method of natural science, i.e., natural observation. The psychiatrist interviews the patient or the psychiatrist will observe the patient on the ward. In each instance, the psychiatrist attempts to understand the nature of the difficulties with which the patient struggles. His major tools are his eyes and ears; his brain is the "computer" that processes these data. His clinical perceptions and his understanding of clinical phenomena enable him to begin to come to some understanding of the data (verbal, motor, cognitive, emotional) presented by the patient. Unlike the psychologist who may wish to study the behavior of the patient in response to standard stimuli, the psychiatrist is more like the anthropologist who studies behavior in its natural context without any intervention. However, motivated by the wish to appear objective, the psychiatrist developed certain standardized techniques through which these observations were being made. The first of such efforts [as by Kempf (1915) and Plant (1922)] were designed to accomplish two things: first, to standardize the observations so that the data from patients could more easily be compared; second, to enable ward personnel (particularly the psychiatric nurse) to make the observations of the patients on the ward for the psychiatrist. These early observational records focused on both the psychiatric and social aspects of the behavior of the patients. Though utilizing increasingly more sophisticated methods of data collection (e.g., scaling techniques), much of the work that followed [which includes the seminal work of such researchers as Thurstone (Thurstone and Thurstone, 1930), Moore (1930), Wittenborn (1950a, b) and Lorr (1953a, b) and the many studies that followed in their footsteps] utilized the same basic paradigm, i.e., the exploration of the wide spectrum of the patient's behavior, hoping that in mining the totality some meaningfulness would emerge.

From this basic model, the research moves in two directions: first, towards increasing comprehensiveness of that which is observed, and second, greater limitedness but specificity. An example of the first direction is the work of Phyllis Wittman (Wittman, 1941). To current behavior (psychiatric and social) she added data regarding the patient's life history [later Phillips (1953) is to develop a scale on the same model]. Cohen *et al.* (1944) had nurses rate such behaviors as activity level, degree of aggressiveness, destructiveness, resistiveness, talkativeness, and tidiness. Malamud *et al.* (1946) had the nurses focus on the patients' appearance, activity level, responsiveness to various people, capacity for attention, direction, their quality of consciousness, speech, thinking, memory, judgment, sexual behavior, mood, emotional behavior, eating, sleeping, and vocational record. Peters (1947) focused on the patients' restlessness, aggressiveness, agitation, affability, mood, feelings. Work by Schofield provided the basis for the work by Lucero and Meyer (1951) who focused on the patients' work behavior, response to meals, to other patients, to psychiatric aides, nurses, doctors, social workers and psychologists, response to various treatment modalities (e.g., electric or insulin shock O.T.), attention to dress, psychomotor activity, speech, and toilet behavior. Rackow *et al.* (1953) tried to systematize the observations of ward personnel in terms of seven scales concerned with the patient's reality testing: emotionality, communication, human relationships, aspiration, intellectual functioning, and general manifest behavior. Guertin and Krugman (1959) similarly focused on the quality of general behavior, interpersonal behavior, emotional behavior, degree of isolation, regressiveness, and reality sense. Sachson *et al.* (1970) focused primarily on the degree of social isolation or involvement on the part of the patient.

An example of the second direction, i.e., of increasing specificity, is that research which began to focus more exclusively on current symptom behavior on the one hand [such as in the work by Bostian *et al.* (1959), Foulds (1965), Jenkins *et al.* (1959), Lorr and Vestre (1969), Nathan (1967), Overall and Gorham (1962), Spitzer *et al.* (1967, 1970), Stone and Skurdal (1968)], or on the patient's behavior as observed on the ward [e.g., Aumack (1962, 1969), Cohen *et al.* (1944), Ferguson *et al.* (1953), Guertin and Krugman (1959), Lorr, O'Connor and Stafford (1960), Lucero and Meyer (1951), Malamud *et al.* (1946), Peters (1947), Rackow *et al.* (1953), Sachson *et al.* (1970)].

The other major modification of the early research has been in the area of data analysis. From a simple scanning of the data to determine the major factors that might have emerged, research workers now utilize factor analysis and other methods of analyzing multifactorial data [e.g., regression equations (as by Lorr, 1953b)].

Because life history, ward behavior, and symptoms are felt to involve different areas of a person's life, in our attempts to explore the behavior subsumed under the various psychiatric diagnoses we will try to look at these various facets of behavior separately. Thus, our analysis of the results of the various studies to be examined will be grouped according to: symptom behavior, general behavior (ordinarily observed on the ward), life history, and the results of psychological testing. Moreover, we plan to look at the data of psychosis and neurosis separately. In all, the system of classification to be examined is the latest one (American Psychiatric Association, 1968). The Manual, therefore, will refer to the manual which presents these data.

CHAPTER 3

PSYCHOTIC REACTIONS

THE Manual divides the psychoses into two major subdivisions: psychoses associated with organic brain syndromes and psychoses not attributable to organic conditions. The former includes psychotic reactions in association with the addictions, infections, CNS deterioration, trauma, neoplasm, and metabolic disorder. The latter includes the schizophrenic reactions, the affective psychoses, and paranoid states.

The question we will be asking here is: to what extent do the various facets of behavior (i.e., symptoms, general current interpersonal behavior, past interpersonal behavior, and behavior in response to psychological test stimuli) support the differentiation of the psychotic reactions as outlined in the Manual?

Although, for example, Diethelm (1953) argues that the term "psychosis" is no longer useful, we find that various kinds of data support the idea of a factor of psychoticism *per se*. Some of the research supported the existence of a factor that clearly could be differentiated from neuroticism. This differentiation was manifest in the analysis of symptoms [e.g., Cottle (1950), Degan (1952), Eysenck (1952b, 1955b), Nathan *et al.* (1968, 1969b), Nathan, Robertson and Andberg (1969), Nathan *et al.* (1969d)], general and current psychiatric and social behavior [e.g., Dawson *et al.* (1958), Hamlin and Lorr (1971), Jenkins and Lorr (1954), Lorr and Vestre (1969), Lorr, Jenkins and O'Connor (1955), Lorr, O'Connor and Stafford (1957), Lorr, Rubinstein and Jenkins (1953), Lorr *et al.* (1962)], life history [e.g., Katz and Lyerly (1963), Trouton and Maxwell (1956)] and re psychological tests [e.g., personality questionnaires: Cattell (1955), Scheier and Cattell (1958), Eysenck and Eysenck (1968), Eysenck, Eysenck and Claridge

(1960), Gough (1946), Guertin and Zilaitis (1953), Meehl and Dahl-strom (1960), Morris (1947), and Wheeler *et al.* (1951); the Rorschach: e.g., Hughes (1950), Haas (1965), and various visuo-motor tasks: e.g., Eysenck (1955a), S. B. G. Eysenck (1956), and Eysenck, Eysenck and Claridge (1960)].

To some extent, therefore, we can see that the data support the notion of a general factor of psychoticism; that clearly seems to exist. Now the question is: to what extent do the data support the notion of greater specificity within the psychotic dimension? One such differen-tiation is the assumption of two major psychotic reactions not associated with organic conditions. One is characterized by bizarreness and disor-ganization of behavior (at all levels, e.g., motoric, affection, and/or cognitive) ordinarily diagnosed as schizophrenia; the other is more characterized not by this quality of disorganization, but reflecting, more, disturbance in the area of mood, feelings, or affect (usually diagnosed as some form of depressive reaction or a reaction against depression, viz., manic behavior). Here, too, from the earliest research endeavors, such a dichotomy of psychotic reactions seems to be validated, as regards general behavior [e.g., Guertin (1952a), Moore (1930), Page *et al.* (1934), and Wittman and Sheldon (1948)], symptoms [e.g., Degan (1952), Monro (1955), Lorr (1957, 1965), Jenkins and Lorr (1954), Lorr and Cave (1966), Lorr and Hamlin (1971), Lorr and O'Connor (1962), Lorr and Vestre (1969), Lorr, Jenkins and O'Connor (1955), Lorr, Klett and Cave (1967), Lorr, Klett and McNair (1963, 1964), Lorr, O'Connor and Stafford (1957, 1960), Lorr, Rubinstein and Jenkins (1953), Lorr *et al.* (1962), Wittenborn (1950a, 1951, 1962), Wittenborn and Bailey (1952), Wittenborn and Holzberg (1951a), Wittenborn and Smith (1964)] and re tests [e.g., Berkowitz and Levine (1953), Thurstone (1934), and Wheeler *et al.* (1951)].

Psychoticism has been found with the Wechsler and MMPI in terms of, in the former, bizarre responses to the questions, in the latter, high scores on the Schizophrenic Scale and low scores on the Ego Strength Scale [e.g., Dahlstrom and Prange (1960), Gough (1946), Guthrie (1950), Meehl (1946), Meehl and Dahlstrom (1960), Rosen (1962), Rubin (1948), Silver and Sines (1961), Wheeler *et al.* (1951), Winne (1951)]. The Rorschach has one measure found to be directly related to psychoticism, viz., form level (F+) [e.g., Beck (1938),

Berkowitz and Levine (1953), Friedman (1952), Guirdham (1937), Hertz and Paolino (1960), Hughes (1950), Kataguchi (1959), Kelley and Klopfer (1939), McReynolds (1951), Piotrowski (1945), Rickers-Ovsiankana (1938), Rieman (1953), Stotsky and Lawrence (1955), Thiesen (1952), Young (1950)].

Thus far, then, we have seen that a factor of psychoticism exists (as differentiated from neuroticism), and within that gross differentiation the data permit us to separate out that which has been called schizophrenia from the so-called affective psychoses. Now, then, the next question we should raise is: just how specific a diagnostic differentiation do these data permit? How close to the (very) specific sub-categories of the Manual do the data permit us to come? One of the big tests (at least in my estimation) is the result of factor analysis. One would presume that if there is some truth to the various diagnostic categories, somewhere in the analysis they will emerge as a factor. Marzolf (1945) had supported this method of data analysis (i.e., factor analysis) that had been developed by Spearman (1929) as a critical procedure to obtain empirical groupings of symptoms. As we shall see, many studies have utilized this method of arriving at "the" factors.

As regards symptoms and general behavior, the pioneering study in this area was done by T. V. Moore (Moore, 1930). He took the data re cognitive functioning (on tests of reasoning, perception, attention and memory), general behavior, and symptoms, intercorrelated each datum with every other, and, through inspection, discerned the factors that emerged. Eight factors appeared in his data:

1. Cognitive deficit.
2. Delusions and hallucinations.
3. Catatonic behavior.
4. Hebephrenic behavior.
5. Retarded depression.
6. What appeared to be a constitutional–hereditary depression.
7. Euphoric mania.
8. Non-euphoric mania.

Interestingly, the data seem to confirm the existence of the two major forms of psychotic reaction, viz., the cognitive disorders and the affective, and they anticipate the findings of later research as regards the process and reactive types of depression. These data also seem to confirm what would appear to be the four major types of schizophrenia, e.g., the undifferentiated, the paranoid, the catatonic, and the hebephrenic, and introduced a novel differentiation (euphoric vs. noneuphoric) of manic reaction (not to be recorded again in later studies). Some years later, Thurstone (1934) applied a formal factor analysis to Moore's data. This analysis produced five factors:

1. Cognitive deficit.
2. Hallucinations.
3. Catatonic behavior.
4. Depression.
5. Manic reaction.

Thurstone's data gave nice support to much of what Moore had arrived at without the aid of a formal factor analysis.

Wittman (Wittman and Sheldon, 1948) analyzed the behavior of the patients at Elgin State Hospital, and found four factors:

1. Schizoid withdrawal.
2. Paranoid projections.
3. Heboid regression.
4. Affective exaggeration.

For some reason, Wittman's data do not reflect the factor of cognitive deficit, but does introduce the more interpersonal style of the schizophrenic. As we will come to see, much of what one gets out of a factor analysis depends on the nature of the data being analyzed; social behavior yields factors of social behavior, cognitive of cognitive, and affective of affective. Wittman's basic data (Wittman, 1941) stressed the interpersonal and not the strictly cognitive; it is for this reason that some of the factors that emerge from the Wittman analysis are different from those that emerged from Moore's.

Of all the many individuals who have conducted studies on the behavior of hospitalized patients in an attempt to explore and/or confirm the kind of syndromes that do exist, the names of two individuals stand out as having involved themselves most heavily in this work, viz., J. R. Wittenborn and Maurice Lorr. We shall, now, explore the nature of the contribution made by their research programs.

In Wittenborn's first (published) study in this area, he developed a 55-item scale of behavior, and explored the factors that emerged from a factor analytic study of the behavior of (140) patients in a state hospital (Connecticut State Hospital). Wittenborn (1950a) found seven factors:

1. Excitement, with delusions and hallucinations.
2. Paranoid schizophrenia.
3. Paranoia without hallucination, but characterized primarily by delusions of persecution.
4. A heboid kind of deterioration.
5. Manic-depressive reaction.
6. Conversion symptoms.
7. Anxiety and depression to a psychotic degree.

From another factor analytic study utilizing this same symptom rating scale (but now using patients from the Northampton V.A. Hospital) Wittenborn (1951) again found seven factors:

1. A factor defined by unawareness of the feelings of others, oppositional behavior, deceptive behavior, assaultive behavior, incontinence, and an inability to stick to a plan—which he felt matched that which was generally subsumed under the diagnosis of simple or undifferentiated schizophrenia.
2. Paranoid schizophrenia with delusions and hallucinations.
3. Paranoid schizophrenia without delusions or hallucinations.
4. A factor described by constant movement, compulsive acts, variation in rate of speech, memory faults, unrecognizable use of words, repudiation of earlier insights, insomnia, obsessions, lack of insight into the behavior of others, loudness, delusions, hallucinations, and incontinence (perhaps similar to the hebephrenic type found before).
5. Manic-depressive reaction.
6. Conversion symptoms.
7. Anxiety.

These seven types seem to be relatively consonant with the symptom types defined by his first study.

In another study at Connecticut State Hospital, Wittenborn (Wittenborn and Holzberg, 1951a) generally reconfirmed the presence of the seven patient types:

1. A factor which he called "deterioration" characterized by: unawareness of the feelings of others, oppositional behavior, deceptive behavior, assaultive behavior, inability to stick to a plan, and incontinence.
2. Catatonic excitement (much like his factor No. 4 of the Northport study).
3. The two forms of paranoia: the one in the form of paranoid schizophrenia,
4. The other in the form of paranoid condition (which lacked the overt symptom of delusions and hallucinations or of cognitive disorder, being characterized by attention-demanding behavior, grandiose notions, excessive planning, exaggeration of ability, and stilted speech).
5. Manic-depressive reaction.
6. Conversion reaction.
7. A syndrome of anxiety (characterized by insomnia, obsessive thinking, phobias, a feeling of doom, anxiety, suicidal attempts, blocking, inability to carry out plans, and delusions of guilt).

In another study, Wittenborn (Wittenborn and Bailey, 1952) found six factors:

1. Patients diagnosed as paranoid, more resembling paranoid schizophrenia.
2. A paranoid schizophrenia with excitement and depression.
3. Agitated depression.
4. Hysteria and depression.
5. Anxiety and depression.
6. A group of patients who were relatively asymptomatic.

Some years later, in a subsequent factor analytic study (Wittenborn, 1962), using a 98-item rating scale with V.A. hospital patients, ten factors emerged:

1. Schizophrenic excitement.
2. Paranoid schizophrenia.
3. Psychotic belligerence.
4. Cognitive impairment.
5. Hebephrenic negativism.
6. Depressive retardation.

7. Conversion reaction.
8. Phobic-compulsive.
9. Anxiety.
10. A factor of homosexuality.

With minor exception, therefore, the analyses of the behavior of hospitalized patients that Wittenborn has conducted over the years tends to eventuate in very similar patterns of behavior, so-called patient types. One should not be too concerned with the relatively minor changes in the number and kinds of factors produced by the different studies; minor changes in the data, in the judges, in the patient populations, and in the mode of data analysis (e.g., when simple structure is assumed and factors are no longer extracted from the matrix) can easily account for such differences. Indeed, in light of such differences that inevitably enter into each study, one is impressed with the degree of consistency there exists from study to study rather than with the differences. Nonetheless, concerned that differences in age of the patients from study to study might produce changes in the symptom clusters, Wittenborn (Wittenborn, Mandler and Waterhouse, 1951) explored the symptom factors produced by 30-year-old as compared to 60-year-old patients. Little difference (except more manifest deterioration in the older group) emerged. Some sex differences, however, were found in symptom clustering [e.g., Wittenborn (1964), Wittenborn and Smith (1964)]. In this vein, it is interesting to note that utilizing a different method of extracting the factors from the matrix made a difference in the outcome. Wittenborn re-analyzed his own data, and whereas the original method of analysis (Wittenborn, 1962) yielded ten factors, the re-analysis of the same data (Wittenborn, 1963) yielded twenty-two (the expansion of factors being accounted for by a decondensing of the traits formerly grouped together, not really novel symptom clusterings). Furthermore, as might be expected, using patients from V.A. mental hygiene clinics (as compared to V.A. hospitals) produced different symptom clusterings [e.g., Lorr, Rubinstein and Jenkins (1953), Lorr and McNair (1963), Lorr, Caffey and Gessner (1968), and Tatom (1958)].

Maurice Lorr began publishing his work soon after Wittenborn. His first rating scale (developed at the Northport V.A. Hospital) consisted of eighty-one scales of behaviors and symptoms (ultimately this was to be called the Inpatient Multidimensional Psychiatric Scale, a scale which, itself, was based on Thurstone's factor analysis of Moore's data, described previously). In an early study (Jenkins and Lorr, 1954) Lorr found six factors:

1. Schizophrenic disorganization.
2. Resistive isolation.
3. Paranoid.
4. Mournful depression.
5. Manic excitement.
6. Panicky agitation with depressive features.

These factors are not unlike those found by Wittenborn. In a study on (423 male) patients drawn from five different V.A. hospitals, utilizing twenty-five raters, Lorr (Lorr, Jenkins and O'Connor, 1955) found eleven factors:

1. Thinking disorder.
2. Perceptual distortion.
3. Resistiveness.
4. Submissive belligerence.
5. Social withdrawal.
6. Bizarre motor behavior.
7. Paranoid schizophrenia.
8. Grandiosity.
9. Manic-depressive reaction.
10. Agitated depression.
11. Activity level.

On the surface, this would appear to be a study which produced a significantly larger number of factors (i.e., patient types) than his earlier study. However, one can see that what in the first study is one factor (i.e., schizophrenic disorganization) is now at least two (i.e., thinking disorder and perceptual distortion); as with the Wittenborn data, the paranoid state has bifurcated into one kind of patient more characteristically diagnosed as paranoid schizophrenic, and a second kind of paranoid where the schizophrenic reaction is not present, although the grandiosity, delusions or hallucinations might be. It is, therefore, possible to conclude that as an artifact of the factors that emerged (perhaps reflecting a slightly different mode of factor analyzing), seemingly new, but not really novel, syndromes have appeared. With minor variation,[1] subsequent studies by Lorr [e.g., Lorr (1957), Lorr, O'Connor and Stafford (1957), Lorr and O'Connor (1962), Lorr et al. (1962), Lorr, Klett and McNair (1964), Lorr (1965), Lorr and Klett (1965), Lorr and Cave (1966), Lorr and Vestre (1969), Lorr and Hamlin (1971)] have replicated the presence of these basic syndromes (or patient types).

As to the studies by other investigators, Degan (1952), for example, factor analyzed the matrix of thirty-two intercorrelated symptoms, eventuating in nine factors:

1. An acute psychotic reaction (characterized by disorganization, disorientation, depression, and hypochondriacal delusions).
2. Hallucinations and delusions.
3. Catatonic behavior.
4. Hebephrenic behavior.
5. Depression.
6. A depressive reaction characterized by sensory deadening with suicidal and homocidal tendencies, and hallucinations.
7. Manic excitement.
8. Irritability and aggressiveness.
9. Neurasthenic, negativistic.

Utilizing a 100-item symptom questionnaire (the Boston City Hospital Behavior Checklist), Nathan [e.g., Nathan et al. (1968)] studying the responses of 605 patients (at Boston City Hospital) found seven basic symptom patterns:

1. Lack of reality testing.
2. Loose associations.
3. Autism.
4. Hallucinations.

---

[1] As, for example, in one study, Lorr (Lorr, O'Connor and Stafford, 1960) found four factors (viz., social withdrawal, thinking disorganization, paranoid belligerence, anxiety and depression), and in another (Lorr, Klett and Cave, 1967), five factors [viz., (excitement, conceptual disorganization, motor disturbance, and grandiosity), (perceptual distortion, grandiosity and expansiveness, and paranoid projection), (hostile belligerence and paranoid projection), (psychomotor retardation, apathy, disorientation, motor disturbances), and (anxiety and intropunitiveness)].

5. Delusions.
6. Anxiety.
7. Compulsions, conversion, phobias.

With the absence of a depressive, manic-depressive, or manic factor (which might be a function of the particular kind of patient that is found in a city hospital versus a state or V.A. hospital), Nathan and Degan's data fit nicely into the symptom patterning that has emerged since Moore's analysis of symptom and behavioral data in the thirties.

It should be of interest for us to note the difference in factors derived when utilizing the same behavioral inventories with, now, out-patient individuals, as compared to hospitalized patients. Using Wittenborn's (1951b) scale, Lorr (Lorr, Rubinstein and Jenkins, 1953) found five factors characterizing the patient types which emerged from the study of V.A. mental hygiene clinic patients:

1. A factor of psychoticism (which included distortions in perception, thinking, and feeling).
2. Agitated depression.
3. Anxiety re somatic concerns.
4. Hostility.
5. Conflicts re sex.

One notes, immediately, the absence of the traditional diagnostic syndromes. This research, however, does not invalidate any of the findings re hospitalized patients. It may mean that we need a different scheme of categorizing different patient populations; it might also mean that these are, simply, different kinds of patients and there is no reason to assume that their behavior should resemble that of hospitalized patients. One might also have to take into consideration that these patients were rated by their therapists who might have an investment (although unconscious) in not seeing their patients' behavior as reflecting severe psychopathology. Whatever the reason, we do note some similarity in the symptom complexes manifested by the out-patient patients as compared to the hospitalized patients, particularly as regards the factors of psychoticism and depression. The different factors reflect what one would imagine to be the different ways of dealing with their problems; rather than the conflicts appearing in the form of paranoid delusions or catatonic behavior, the outpatient patients reflect concern regarding their body, sex, and manifest hostility. On a follow-up study of the Lorr study, Tatom (1958) selected five patients from each of the following diagnostic categories: hysteric, anxiety state, obsessive-compulsive neurosis, and schizophrenia. The rated behavior of these (V.A.) mental hygiene clinic patients showed little correlation between the symptoms patterns they revealed and those found in the traditional diagnostic schema. The factors that did emerge were:

1. Ambulatory paranoid schizophrenia.
2. Conversion hysteria.
3. Intrapunitive type.
4. Passive-dependent type.

In another study, Lorr (Lorr and McNair, 1963) used a more inter-personally oriented behavior inventory [developed by Leary and Coffey (1955)]. The factors derived from the ratings by their therapists were:

1. Dominance.
2. Hostile-rebelliousness.
3. Suspicious.
4. Inhibited.
5. Intropunitive.
6. Need for nurturance.
7. Affiliative.
8. Sociable.

In that the basic data are different (i.e., the focus on interpersonal behavior exclusively) it is not surprising that the factors that do emerge are different from that found in the traditional psychiatric categories (which are not predicated on interpersonal interactions). In a follow-up to this study, Lorr (McNair and Lorr, 1965) used the same inter-personal behavior inventory to study the responses of (450 V.A.) mental hygiene clinic patients rated by their therapists. Eleven factors emerged, seven of the factors that were found before:

1. Dominance.
2. Hostility.

3. Mistrust.
4. Intropunitiveness.
5. Need for nurturance.
6. Need for affiliation.
7. Sociability.

Plus:

8. Detachment.
9. Passive dependency.
10. Need for succorance.
11. Exhibitionism.

The additional factors seem reasonable addenda to the original seven, and may simply reflect differences in the patient population.

In another study, Lorr (Lorr, Caffey and Gessner, 1968) took seventy-seven items from the MMPI (which, in some regard, is a behavioral inventory, only with the individual "rating" himself on the various items). The patient types that emerged from the data from patients from a V.A. mental hygiene clinic were:

1. Autism.
2. Depression with anxiety.
3. Somatic symptoms.
4. Suspiciousness.
5. Resentment.
6. Tension.
7. Introversion.

The symptom clusterings that emerge from the analysis of the current behavior of out-patient patients not only bears little resemblance to the clusterings emerging from the analysis of the behavior of hospitalized patients, but also does not reveal the clusterings found in the Manual. The behavior of the patients in the clinics, as compared to those in hospitals, reveals less pethology of a psychotic kind, being seemingly more neurotic.

As regards case history data, Wittenborn and Lesser (1951) (studying the records of patients from Connecticut State Hospital) factor analyzed these data, and found eight factors:

1. A tendency towards physical assaultiveness.
2. Social withdrawal.

3. Those who cried easily.
4. Agitation.
5. Depression.
6. Suicidal attempts.
7. Guilt over sex.
8. Insomnia.

Other studies [e.g., Sherman and Kraines (1943), Trouton and Maxwell (1956), Pokorny (1962)] have demonstrated that the life histories of schizophrenics *are* different from those of other individuals manifesting other forms of psychopathology. However, it is clear, as from the study by Wittenborn and Lesser, that the factors that emerge from an analysis of behavior as derived from case history do not resemble those that emerge from the analysis of current behavior. We shall make more of this later.

CHAPTER 4

SCHIZOPHRENIA

WE have already seen (in Chapter 3) that the data support the idea of a cognitive disorder as distinct from affective disorders. Now the question is how much more specificity in sub-grouping the data do permit.

Because of the enormity of the problems associated with schizophrenia, because of the amount of clinical and research time and energy that has gone into trying to understand this phenomenon of psychic nature, I felt it justified to focus on the degree to which the data support the existence of the diagnostic categories within the major problem of psychiatry: schizophrenia. We will, in the next chapter, have the opportunity to explore the nature of the affective disorders.)

The Manual lists fifteen sub-types of schizophrenia, amongst those being:

Simple type.
Hebephrenic type.
Catatonic type.
Paranoid type.
Schizoaffective type.
Acute reaction.
Chronic reaction.
Childhood type.
Latent type.
Residual type.
"Other" (and "unspecified") type.

Going back to the original data by Moore (1930), of the eight factors he determined existed in his correlational matrix (of symptoms, behavior, and tests of cognitive functioning), four related to schizophrenia:

1. A factor of cognitive deficit.
2. Delusional-hallucinating.
3. Catatonia.
4. Hebephrenia.

Seemingly, therefore, Moore's data seem to confirm a general factor of schizophrenicity, i.e., the cognitive disorder (that is, a patient type where the cognitive disorder is prominent or predominant) and three other patient types, quite consistent with the traditional types generally diagnosed, although not supporting the existence of all the types outlined in the Manual. In the more formal factoring of Moore's data (Thurstone, 1934), of the five factors Thurstone's analysis extracted, three were related to schizophrenia:

1. A factor of cognitive disorder.
2. Catatonia.
3. A hallucinatory group.

Of the factors Phyllis Wittman was able to extract from her data (Wittman and Sheldon, 1948), three were relevant to schizophrenia:

1. Schizoid withdrawal.
2. Paranoid projection.
3. Heboid regression.

In several studies, Wittenborn [Wittenborn (1950a, 1951, 1962, 1963), Wittenborn and Bailey (1952), Wittenborn and Holzberg (1951a)] has been able to demonstrate the consistency of a paranoid, a catatonic, and a hebephrenic form of schizophrenia, much as Lorr's studies have demonstrated [e.g., Lorr, Wittman and Schanberger (1951), Jenkins and Lorr (1954), Lorr and Jenkins (1953), Lorr, Jenkins and O'Connor (1955), Lorr (1957), Lorr, O'Connor and Stafford (1957, 1960), Lorr and O'Connor (1962), Lorr *et al.* (1962), McNair and Lorr (1965), Lorr, Klett and McNair (1964), Lorr (1965), Lorr and Cave (1966), Lorr, Klett and Cave (1967), Lorr and Vestre (1969), Lorr and Hamlin (1971), Hamlin and Lorr (1971)] the factors of: cognitive disorganization, social withdrawal, and a paranoid and hebephrenic reaction types.

In a series of studies analyzing the behavior of various forms of schizophrenia, Guertin found several consistencies. In one study (Guertin, 1952a), Guertin found the following factors:

1. Excitement–hostility.
2. Retardation and withdrawal.
3. Confusion and withdrawal.
4. Personality disorganization.
5. Persecutory suspiciousness.
6. Guilt conflicts.

In another study (Guertin and Jenkins, 1956), he found:

1. Degree of schizophrenicity.
2. Withdrawal.
3. Disorganization.
4. Agitation and anxiety.

In another study (Guertin and Krugman, 1959), he found the factors of:

1. Deteriorated behavior.
2. Regressive agitation.
3. Reality concern.
4. Interpersonal tensions.
5. Emotional control.
6. Isolation.

With regard to the behavior of chronic schizophrenics, Guertin(1955a, b, 1956a) found in addition to social withdrawal and cognitive disorganization, apathy, factors which were also found by Wing (1961) in his analysis of the behavior of his sample of chronic schizophrenics.

It would appear that in comparison to the work of Wittenborn and Lorr, Guertin's work tends to focus on various *facets* of the schizophrenic reaction. On the other hand, the data of Wittenborn and Lorr seem to reflect patient *types* (which only a few of Guertin's studies do— e.g., Guertin, 1952b, 1961). The work of many other workers [e.g., Cohen *et al.* (1966), Gard and Bendig (1964), Gurel (1967), Honigfeldt and Klett (1965), Katz and Cole (1963), Pugh and Ray (1965)] tends to reflect behavior dimensions much like that of Guertin, whereas others (e.g., Degan, 1952) seem to reflect the patient types à la Wittenborn and Lorr. Although these two sets of findings might seem contradictory and/ or confusing, they can be explained in terms of the nature of the scales utilized. Undoubtedly, the scales utilized by Guertin focused on different aspects of behavior than those utilized by Wittenborn and Lorr, hence the differences in the outcome of their studies. Therein, we will focus on later on, lies one of the major difficulties of research in this area, viz., a shift in focus of the behavior being analyzed, and seemingly different factors emerge. Moreover, a shift in the patient population produces its changes in the outcomes of the studies as well. Take, for example, Guertin's studies using chronic patients, or Nathan's, using patients from a city hospital, as compared to the patients from the V.A. or a state hospital, as employed in the studies by Wittenborn and Lorr. In this regard, the analysis of the behaviour of individuals being seen in outpatient clinics [e.g., as by Lorr and McNair (1963), Lorr, Caffey and Gessner (1968), Lorr, Rubinstein and Jenkins (1953), Tatom (1958)] reflect a factor of schizophrenia, but do not reflect the typical patient subtypes as the data from the hospitalized samples do.

Though the above research tends to lend support to the traditional sub-types of schizophrenia, other research, e.g., that by Freudenberg and Robertson (1956) and Zigler and Phillips (1961a), using their scales on hospitalized patients as well, do not.

The research by Peter Nathan (e.g., Nathan *et al.*, 1968) revealed:

1. The symptoms one would expect to find in psychotic states (e.g., hallucinations, delusions, lack of reality testing, looseness of association, autism).
2. That anxiety appeared in all states of psychopathology.
3. That symptoms which tend to characterize neurotics (e.g., obsessive compulsive behavior and phobias) were seen in *all* states of psychopathology, neurotic *and* psychotic.
4. That the current diagnostic procedures permit the reliable differentiation of a general psychotic state from a general neurotic one.

Seven basic symptom complexes (patient types) emerged from the analysis of his data:

1. Hallucinations.
2. Delusions.
3. Lack of reality testing.
4. Autism.
5. Loose associations.
6. Anxiety.
7. Compulsions, conversions, phobias.

In subsequent research (Nathan *et al.*, 1969c), Nathan found that although thought disorder seems to be characteristic of psychotic states in general, more characteristic of functional states, and somewhat more characteristic of schizophrenic, in his sample, even some of his neurotics also seemed to reveal the presence of a thought disorder. Flight of ideas and retardation (i.e. speed of thinking) is a factor characteristic of both the manics and the hebephrenics; delusions and hallucinations seem unique to psychotic states; difficulty in retention of ideas are more characteristic of organic states. Nathan (Nathan, Robertson and Andberg, 1969) also found that depression and anxiety are not unique to any diagnostic group, and that abnormal affect is not only characteristic of schizophrenics, but some of the individuals in his sample diagnosed as neurotic, as well.

A factor analysis of behavioral data by Grinker (Grinker, Werble and Drye, 1968) supports the idea of a latent or borderline type. However, in these data, we see that what we call "borderline" seems to fall on a continuum of difficulties between psychosis and neurosis, but into four seemingly relatively distinct categories along that continuum, i.e.:

1. That which borders, behaviorally and emotionally, on a true psychotic condition, characterized by:
   (a) clinically inappropriate (but transient) behavior;
   (b) negativism towards others;
   (c) careless in personal grooming;
   (d) erratic sleep and eating patterns;
   (e) occasional outbursts of impulsive anger;
   (f) depression.

2. What Grinker *et al.* call the "core borderline syndrome" characterized by:
   (a) negativism;
   (b) minimal involvement with others.

3. The "as if" person, characterized by:
   (a) bland, adaptive behavior;
   (b) little negative affects, but also little positive;
   (c) no evidence for love for anybody or anything;
   (d) poor sense of self.

4. A group whose behavior (i.e., childlike, clinging depression and dependency) places it contiguous to the more classical neurotic reaction.[2]

In comparing the life histories of patients diagnosed from the various subgroups of schizophrenia, one finds that the life histories of individuals in these various subgroups are not significantly different, one from the other [e.g., Wittenborn and Lesser (1951), Zigler and Phillips (1961b), Frank (1965), Gunderson and Arthur (1968)].

In looking more specifically at the various subgroups of schizophrenia, some studies [e.g., Foulds and Owen (1963), Katz, Cole and Lowery (1964)] found that the behavior of some paranoids differs significantly from that of others (i.e., a paranoid is not a paranoid is not a paranoid). Thus Foulds and Owen found that their data could differentiate between the integrated and non-integrated paranoid person: the poorly integrated were younger, experienced delusions of grandeur, and directed their hostility outward (i.e., were extra-punitive). The data from the study by Katz, Cole, and Lowery revealed three different patterns of behavior being subsumed under the category of paranoia: a person who is hostile and belligerent, a person who is anxious, intropunitive, who utilizes projection, and, hence, demonstrates perceptual distortions, and a third person who is characterized by excitement, hostile belligerence and grandiose expansiveness. Thus, although all three types of persons carried the same diagnosis, viz., paranoid schizophrenia, it is apparent that they are not quite the same sort of individuals psychologically. On the other hand, e.g., Wittman and Steinberg (1944), Gorham and Overall (1961) failed to find significant differences in the behavior patterns of schizophrenics diagnosed as paranoid from those that were not. And Bonner and Kent (1936) found it difficult to differentiate the excitement of catatonics from that of manics.

Data from some research [as summarized in, e.g., Herron (1962) and Kantor and Herron (1966)] strongly suggest that a more significant,

---

[2] Though not reflecting the specificity of the subcategories within the borderline range, psychological tests certainly go along with the concept of a range of psychopathology which stands somewhere in between psychosis and neurosis, manifesting characteristics of each. [For a review of the research re the borderline on psychological tests see Frank (1970).]

consistent (and, as we shall see, more meaningful) differentiation that emerges from the life styles of schizophrenics rather than the traditional subtypes is the process-reactive types.

Now we will explore the data as derived from psychological tests. Because of the tremendous number of tests that exist, we must be selective in our exploration. I have, therefore, decided to restrict our exploration to those tests used most extensively in clinical and research studies in psychopathology, viz., the MMPI, the Rorschach, and the adult form of the Wechsler. Use of these tests will also enable us to compare the data derived from a relatively structured personality test (the MMPI) that of a relatively unstructured one (the Rorschach), and more clearly tests of personality (the MMPI and the Rorschach) with that of an assessment of various cognitive functions (the Wechsler).

With regard to data gathered via the MMPI, most of the research has been rather consistent in demonstrating the ability to differentiate the pattern of responses of schizophrenics from that of other non-schizophrenic groups of patients [e.g., Rosen (1958), Silver and Sines (1961), Taulbee and Sisson (1957)]. On the other hand, Schmidt (1945) found that in his data although all psychiatric groups were clearly differentiated from normals, there was considerable overlap in the patterns of responses of most psychiatric groups.

In their factor analysis of patients' responses to the Schizophrenia Scale of the MMPI, Comrey and Marggraff (1958) did not find the resultant clusters of responses to fall into the traditional subtypings. Rather, their factor analysis resulted in ten factors, viz.:

1. Paranoid ideas.
2. Difficulty in concentrating.
3. Poor physical health.
4. Psychotic tendencies.
5. Feelings of rejection.
6. Withdrawal.
7. Father identification.
8. Concern with sexual matters.
9. Items reflecting repression.
10. Mother identification.

From this one might conclude that either the Schizophrenia Scale is not a "pure" scale and is contaminated by "extraneous" (to schizophrenia) factors, or (since the Scale was originally developed on the basis of the responses of patients diagnosed as schizophrenic) the data of the MMPI do not demonstrate that the responses of schizophrenics cluster into groupings defined by the various traditional subtypes, *or* that there *are* subtypes of schizophrenia, but they do not resemble the traditional subtypes. It is possible that the Schizophrenia Scale of the MMPI taps into psychiatric (i.e., symptom) *and* psychological problems simultaneously, hence the kinds of factors extracted from the Scale.

In a factor analysis of the responses of a variety of patients to selected items of the MMPI, Lorr (Lorr, Caffey and Gessner, 1968) found seven symptom complexes to emerge; of these, only two referred to schizophrenic reactions:

1. Autism.
2. Suspiciousness.

Analysis of the data as regards patients diagnosed as paranoid, some research [e.g. Kleinmuth (1960), Petzel and Gynther (1969)] indicates that the MMPI data do not differentiate between schizophrenics who have been diagnosed as paranoid and those who have not. Other research [e.g., Comrey and Marggraff (1958), Guertin and Zilaitis (1953)] suggests that there may be more than one kind of paranoid. The factor analytic study of the MMPI responses of patients diagnosed as paranoid schizophrenic done by Guertin and Zilaitis indicated that there were at least three different clusterings within the paranoid grouping, viz., an overtly delusional type, a well-integrated type, and a person who is, primarily, hypersensitive, inadequate, and withdrawn.

With regard to the data from the Rorschach: one dimension that does seem to be consistent with regard to the performance of schizophrenics is poor form level (i.e., poorly perceived and conceived, inaccurate responses) [e.g., Beck (1938), Berkowitz and Levine (1953), Friedman (1952), Guirdham (1937), Hertz and Paolino (1960), Hughes (1950), Kataguchi (1959), Kelley and Klopfer (1939), McReynolds

(1951), Piotrowski (1945), Rickers-Ovsiankana (1938), Rieman (1953), Stotsky and Lawrence (1955), Thiesen (1952), Young (1950)]. There is also some evidence that indicates that schizophrenics also tend to be unable to deal effectively with color [e.g., Beck (1938), Hertz and Paolino (1960), Kelley and Klopfer (1939), Rickers-Ovsiankana (1938), Taulbee et al. (1956), Thiesen (1952), Vinson (1960) and Weiner (1961, 1964)], as well as manifesting unusual content in their responses [e.g., Bower et al. (1960), Hertz and Paolino (1960), Kelley and Klopfer (1939), Rickers-Ovsiankana (1938), Rieman (1953), Thiesen (1952), Vinson (1960)]. There are, also, other studies which ended up with the schizophrenic *not* revealing any characteristic performance on the Rorschach [e.g., Bendig and Hamlin (1955), Bradway and Heisler (1953), Hackfield (1935), Klinger and Roth (1964), Knopf (1956), Mensh and Matarazzo (1954), Molish (1951), Sisson et al. (1956), Wertheimer (1953), and Wittenborn and Holzberg (1951b)].

Several investigators have devised complex ratios with each Rorschach factor contributing a special amount to the overall score [e.g., Piotrowski and Lewis (1950), Powers and Hamlin (1955), and Kataguchi (1959)]. Too little work, however, has been conducted with these ratios for their value to be evaluated here.

Dimmick (1935) compared the performance of hebephrenics with that of paranoids and those diagnosed as simple schizophrenics. Hebephrenics proved to be different (lower) on form level (i.e., manifested more poorly delineated percepts), use of color, and higher on the presence of unusual organization of the blot. The paranoids were different than those diagnosed as simple schizophrenic on virtually the same dimensions (perhaps suggesting some gradation of ego pathology with regard to these groups). On the other hand, Friedman (1952) could not find much on the Rorschach which differentiated his samples of catatonics and hebephrenics, one from the other. A telling piece of research was done by Sam Beck (Beck, 1954). His factor analytic study of test and behavioral data produced six different clusterings, but these did not match the traditional groupings. His factors reflected two types of schizophrenia that were found in childhood (one with labile affect, the other characterized by withdrawal), two chronic types (one characterized by intellectual deterioration, the other by excessive use of fantasy), a type characterized by a defensive exterior, but with a brittle interior, and a type characterized by a stabilized schizophrenic pattern (what Rapaport would call a schizophrenic character).

With regard to the Wechsler test: as compared to normals and other psychiatric groups, the performance of the schizophrenics was characterized by greater inter- and intra-test variability in many of the research studies [e.g., Weider (1943), Rabin (1944a, b), Olch (1948), Klein (1948), Holzberg and Deane (1950), Trehub and Scherer (1958)]. Yet there is research which refutes this finding [e.g., Gilliland et al. (1945), Magaret and Wright (1943), Watson (1965a, b)]. Some research seems to suggest that the schizophrenic's thought disorder is more clearly reflected in the performance of tasks requiring verbalization, particularly such as Vocabulary [e.g., Babcock (1930), Hausmann (1933), Kraus (1965), and Moran et al. (1952a, b), and on the basis of the work done by Feifel (1949) and Jones (1957, 1959), Hunt, Schwartz and Walker (1965) developed a scale of schizophrenicity based on an analysis of answers to Vocabulary]. And whereas some research suggests that schizophrenics reveal a characteristic performance on the subtests so that a significant and identifiable pattern emerges [e.g., Rabin (1941, 1942), Magaret (1942), Rapaport et al. (1945), Rogers (1951)], there are a number of studies which refute this notion [e.g., Brecher (1946), Cohen (1952), Frank et al. (1955), Frank (1956), Garfield (1948, 1949), Harper (1950), Johnson (1949), Kogan (1950), Levine (1949), Olch (1948), Wittenborn (1949)]. Indeed, factor analytic studies of Wechsler data [e.g., by Cohen (1952) and Frank (1956)] do not demonstrate that the factors which are generated have anything to do with psychiatric groupings. Consistently, the factors which have emerged have been defined by three factors: the tests have grouped themselves according to those dealing, primarily, with verbal material, nonverbal material, and tests of distractibility.

Let us, now, try to summarize that which we can glean from the studies on schizophrenia. In the first place, let us remind ourselves of the data in the Manual. If we can permit ourselves to ignore two of the "types" delineated therein, the "residual" and "other", and if we permit ourselves to see acuteness and chronicity not as types, as the Manual tends to do, but as qualitative states of any schizophrenic reaction, then we can see that the Manual presents us with seven basic subtypes:

1. Simple.
2. Catatonic.
3. Paranoid.
4. Hebephrenic.
5. Schizoaffective.
6. Latent.
7. Childhood type.

The question remains as to how the data of the studies relate to these subtypes.

As regards an analysis of current symptoms and behavior, the factors that seem to appear in the majority of the studies are two of the major characteristics of the schizophrenic reaction, viz., cognitive disorder and withdrawal from social interaction. The data do, however, support the presence of four of the seven subtypes listed in the Manual:

1. Paranoid.
2. Catatonic.
3. Hebephrenic.
4. Latent.

Analysis of past behavior (through case histories) tends to reveal factors comprised of social behavior and reflecting patients' social isolation and disorganization. These data, however, do not cluster into groupings reflective of the subtypes. That is, no behavioral pattern revealed in the life histories is characteristic of any of the traditional subtypes.

As far as the data from the psychological tests are concerned: here, too, we note that although the essential difficulties characteristic of schizophrenia, *sui generis*, emerge, the patients' responses to the three tests we explored (i.e., the MMPI, the Rorschach, and the Wechsler) did not cluster into groups resembling or consonant with the traditional subtypes. And, moreover, the research suggests that at least one of the subtypes, viz., paranoid schizophrenia, may be a much more complicated syndrome than we conceived. The data suggest that what has been subsumed under one diagnostic category: paranoid schizophrenia, may be at least three different groups of individuals: an overtly delusional person, a well-integrated person who utilizes projection as a major mechanism, and a person who is primarily hypersensitive, with strong feelings of inadequacy, who retreats from interpersonal relations.

It seems clear that as regards schizophrenia, only the symptoms conform to any degree to the traditional subtypes; the data from life history and psychological tests do not. Another way of saying this is that the traditional subtypes of schizophrenia define only current symptom pictures; they offer no information as regards past life behavior or performance on psychological tests. An important dimension that emerges from some research, defining types which seem more meaningful than the traditional subtypes, is the process-reactive differentiation [e.g., see Herron (1962) and Kantor and Herron (1966) for a review of this research].

CHAPTER 5

DEPRESSIVE REACTIONS

THE Manual lists three major forms of depressive reaction:

1. Involutional melancholia.
2. Manic-depressive psychosis.
3. Depressive neurosis.

Mindful of the differences between hopelessness (Melges and Bowlby, 1969), grief (Parkes, 1965a, b), and despair, it is clear that the clinical judgment that there *is* a form of psychological disorder (not just a mood or feeling state) which has an integrity of its own, separate and distinct from, e.g., schizophrenia, has validity. A factor of depression has been found in almost every factor analytic study of symptom behavior.[3] In terms of the differentiation between a depressive reaction and a schizophrenic reaction, analyses of data indicate that ordinarily in the depressive, regardless of how psychotic he or she might become, there is not the same quality of thought disorder as one finds in the schizophrenic.[4]

---

[3] From the earliest analysis of such data [e.g., Moore (1930) and Thurstone (1933)] to the more current [e.g., Cattell (1955, 1956), Cattell *et al.* (1954b), Comrey (1957b), Degan (1952), Eysenck (1952a), S. B. G. Eysenck (1956), Freudenberg and Robertson (1956), Harrow *et al.* (1966), Jenkins and Lorr (1954), Katz (1965), Katz and Lyerly (1963), Klein (1967), Lorr (1957, 1965), Lorr and Cave (1966), Lorr and Hamlin (1971), Lorr and Klett (1965), Lorr and O'Connor (1962), Lorr, Jenkins and O'Connor (1955), Lorr, Klett and Cave (1967), Lorr, Klett and McNair (1964), Lorr *et al.* (1962), Overall (1963), Overall and Hollister (1965), Scheier and Cattell (1958), Vestre (1966), Vestre and Zimmerman (1970), Wittenborn (1950b, 1951, 1962, 1963), Wittenborn and Bailey (1952), Wittenborn and Holzberg (1951a), Wittenborn and Lesser (1951), Wittenborn and Weiss (1952), Wittenborn, Holzberg and Simon (1953), Wittenborn, Mandler and Waterhouse (1951)].

[4] Part of the problem in diagnostic differentiation stems from the fact that a depressive reaction can be masked (Lesse, 1968) or might mask a more serious (i.e., schizophrenic) disorder (Mercer, 1949), that depressiveness is not uniquely character-

35

In terms of the extent to which the research supports the clinical notions of the *forms* of depression, as embodied in the Manual, we note that the research confirms that there is, on the one hand, a psychotic and a neurotic form of depression [e.g., Beigel and Murphy (1971), Beigel *et al.* (1971), Blinder (1966), Degan (1952), Friedman *et al.* (1963), Katz and Lyerly (1963), Kay *et al.* (1969), Lorr, Jenkins and O'Connor (1955), Lorr, O'Connor and Stafford (1957)] and a bi-polar (i.e., manic-depressive, cyclothymic) as well as uni-polar form of depressive reaction [e.g., Beigel and Murphy (1971a, b), Kraeplin (1921), Lorr, Jenkins and O'Connor (1955), Lorr, O'Connor and Stafford (1957), Wittenborn (1950b, 1951), Wittenborn and Holzberg (1951a)].

However, as one looks closer at these data, the rather deceptive simplicity of depressive reactions disappears. One notes that depressiveness also manifests itself in at least two different psychological modalities, viz., in terms of either mood or psychomotor behavior [e.g., Beigel and Murphy (1971a, b), Cropley and Weckowicz (1966), Friedman *et al.* (1963), Hamilton and White (1959), Katz (1965), Kraeplin (1921), Lorr, Klett and Cave (1967), Lorr, Klett and McNair (1964), Lorr, Sonn and Katz (1967), Overall (1963), Overall *et al.* (1966), Raskin *et al.* (1967)], with the probability being that there are some depressive states characterized by the mood factor almost exclusively, some by psychomotor manifestations, with minimum awareness of the depressive mood and all combinations along a continuum of somato-

---

istic of *any* psychological disorder, and may pervade the clinical picture of *any* form of psychological disturbance [e.g., Klerman and Paykel (1970), Mahrer and Bernstein (1969), Wittenborn and Lesser (1951)]; certainly, suicidal thoughts or actions are not unique to any one diagnostic group [e.g., Pokerny (1960, 1964), Temoche *et al.* (1964)], and that there is a form of depressive reaction which reflects the characteristics of depressiveness *and* schizophrenia concurrently [e.g., Wittenborn and Weiss (1952)]. The most characteristic and distinguishing feature of the depressive reactions, as compared to schizophrenia, is the absence of a primary thought disorder [e.g., Lewis and Piotrowski (1954)]. On the other hand, Lipkin *et al.* (1970) found that although schizophrenics or manics in excitement could not be differentiated clinically, they could by response to lithium carbonate, and Greenblatt *et al.* (1964) found that neurotic depressives, manic-depressives, and involutional depressives tend to respond differently to various psychiatric treatments. For example, involutional, manic-depressive, and schizophrenics with depression respond well to ECT; neurotic depressives tend not to. Neurotic depressives improve in response to almost any kind of treatment, but particularly well to Nardil (but also placebo).

psychic manifestations in between. Furthermore, the data indicate that there seems to be a process and reactive form of depression much as we have seen exists in schizophrenia [e.g., Blinder (1966), Carney et al. (1965), Gillespie (1929), Hill (1968), Kay et al. (1969), Kiloh and Garside (1963), Kiloh et al. (1962), Lewis (1934), Mendels (1965, 1968), Moore (1930), Rose (1963), Rosenthal and Gudeman (1967), Rosenthal and Klerman (1966), Roth (1960), Sandifer et al. (1966), even though some analyses of data fail to confirm this dichotomy, e.g., McConaghy et al. (1967) and Mendels and Cochrane (1968)]. A partial test of the validity of these latter dimensions is the fact that the reactive and process types respond differentially to various forms of psychiatric treatment [e.g., to chemotherapy: Barbato (1942), Greenblatt et al. (1964), Kiloh et al. (1962); or ECT: Carney et al. (1965), Greenblatt et al. (1964), Mendels (1965), Rose (1965); or psychotherapy: Arieti (1962), Roth (1960)]. Indeed, as we analyze depressive reactions, taking into consideration all possible facets of behavior (i.e., cognitive, affective, and behavioral), one finds, as did Kraeplin (1921), that there are depressive reactions with (or without) motor excitement, with (or without) anxiety, and with (or without) loss of energy and psychomotor retardation. Moreover, factor analyses of the total behavior of the depressive have almost consistently yielded four to six factors presumably defining different types of depressive reactions.

Grinker (and his associates) conducted two studies on depression. In the first (Grinker et al., 1961), he found depressives falling into five rather separate groups, vi .:

1. The dismal, hopeless, self-castigating person.
2. The person who feels equally as dismal and hopeless, but attributes his or her depression to external events or persons.
3. A person with strong guilt feelings regarding aggression.
4. Depression accompanied by marked agitation or anxiety.
5. A clinging, demanding, angry person.

In the second study (Grinker and Nunnally, 1965) five other factors were found:

1. A person characterized by hopelessness, helplessness, a sense of failure, unworthiness, guilt, internal suffering.
2. A person concerned with material loss.

3. A person obsessed with guilt over wrongdoing and the wish to make restitution.
4. A depressiveness without anxiety.
5. A person characterized by feelings of envy, loneliness, martyred affliction, one who seems to derive a considerable amount of secondary gain from the illness, and one who attempts to provoke a sense of guilt in others to force the world to make redress.

Friedman *et al.* (1963) found four types of depression:

1. A retarded, withdrawn, apathetic type.
2. A depressive with feelings of guilt, loss of self-esteem, doubting, internalizing.
3. An agitated, demanding, hypochondriacal type.
4. A depressive characterized by physiological factors, e.g., loss of appetite, sleep disturbances, constipation, loss of satisfaction in work.

Cropley and Weckowicz (1966), administering Beck's Inventory of Depression (Beck *et al.*, 1961), found six types:

1. A person characterized by a sense of punishment and guilt feelings.
2. Psychomotor retardation.
3. Negative body image, self-punishment, pessimism, crying.
4. Dissatisfaction with self (self-accusation, self-hate, a sense of failure).
5. A sense of failure and lack of satisfaction but absence of sleep disturbances, crying, or indecisiveness.
6. Irritability, somatic preoccupation, indecisiveness, self-hate.

In another study, Weckowicz, Muir and Copley (1967), again using the Beck Inventory, the analysis produced three types of depressive patients, those with:

1. Guilt.
2. Psychomotor retardation.
3. Somatic disturbances.

Overall *et al.* (1966), using the Brief Psychiatric Rating Scale (Overall and Gorham, 1962), found symptoms clustering into three different types of depressives; depressives with:

1. Anxiety.
2. Hostility.
3. Psychomotor retardation.

Lorr, Sonn and Katz (1967) found five different depressive types:

1. A depressed person characterized by anxiety and self-blame.
2. Depression accompanied by impairment of ability to function in life.
3. Psychomotor retardation.
4. Depression with somatic symptoms.
5. A person with just a depressed mood.

Raskin *et al.* (1967) found depressives differentially associated with:

1. Loss of interest and involvement in activities.
2. Hostility.
3. Feelings of guilt and unworthiness.
4. Anxiety and tension.
5. Sleep disturbances.
6. Somatic complaints.
7. Psychomotor retardation.
8. Depressive mood.
9. Conceptual disorganization.

As we did when we explored the data with regard to the diagnosis of schizophrenia, we will, now, look at the performance of the depressive on tests, looking intensively, in particular, at the performance of the depressive where we would expect the unique quality of their personality to appear most clearly, i.e., the personality tests, viz., the Rorschach and the MMPI. Here, we have studies by Levy and Beck (1934), Guirdham (1936a, b), Varvel (1941), Young (1950) and Kobler and Stiel (1953) to review.

The Rorschach performance of those individuals diagnosed as depressive reveals a remarkable consistency. As regards depressiveness, *per se*, the studies all seem to point to diminished responsiveness in general, and, more specifically, reduced responsiveness to color and movement. (I am tempted to say the data suggest that the *élan vital*, the life force, is gone.) Psychotic depressions are differentiated from neurotic primarily in terms of the degree to which these (above) elements are present or not, and the degree to which the factor of psychoticism (i.e., alienation from reality) becomes reflected in responses of poor form. People with involutional depression seem to be different from the "ordinary" depressive, whether neurotic or psychotic. Young, and Kobler and Stiel studied the response style of involutionals. As distinguished from the "usual" depressive, the involutional demonstrated contamination of the form quality of the percepts, stereotypy, and a greater tendency to respond with original responses (making them resemble, psychologically, the schizophrenic). Kobler and Stiel concluded, however, that the better way to differentiate the involutional from the other depressives was qualitatively (i.e., the content of the responses), rather than regarding the quantitative parameters of the Rorschach.

As regards the MMPI, as we know, one of the so-called "clinical scales" D, was developed to detect depression. Hathaway and McKinley (1942) note that the D scale not only sorts out people with clear-cut depressive illness, but cuts across psychiatric categories to identify anyone with depressive affect. The experience with the D scale is that it *is* responsive to depression and does identify degrees of depressiveness. Interestingly, of the sixty items of the depression scale, factor analysis (Comrey, 1957b) identifies only eight of these as reflecting depressive mood. Therefore, the depression scale of the MMPI seems to be a complex set of items, not only reflecting the complexity of the scale, but, also, the several facets of depression. The factor analysis of the D scale by Comrey noted that the scale seemed to be composed of eight dimensions. Aside from the eight items reflecting depressive mood, the other factors were: neuroticism, repression, cynicism, religious fervor, poor physical health, euphoria, and hostility. O'Connor *et al.* (1957) factor analyzed the responses to the D scale and found that it sorted out into factors of:

1. Hypochondriasis.
2. Cycloid tendencies.
3. Hostility.

4. Feelings of inferiority.
5. Mood.

It seems safe to assume that there may be several different kinds of depression, or perhaps another way of speaking about the result of these factor analytic studies is that there are several aspects of depressive illness, these factors identifying them, or that there are several ways in which depression can manifest itself. Whatever the "correct" way of stating the results in psychological terms, these factors seem to have little to do with the neurotic–psychotic dimension, the uni- or bi-polar aspect, or the process–reactive (i.e., endogenous–exogenous) differentiations.

In summary, what the research in the area of depression does seem to indicate is that to some extent the data (both behavior and test) support some of the aspects of the traditional diagnostic schema (particularly the neurotic and psychotic differentiation), and the behavioral data support the idea of uni-polar and bi-polar forms of depression. The behavioral data also suggest that there may be a process and reactive form of depressive reaction much as there is in schizophrenia. Both behavioral and test data suggest that there may be several basic constellations of symptoms involved in depressiveness, e.g., the degree to which the depression has a somatic component or, rather, the degree to which the depressive affect has been translated (transformed) into the language of the body, the degree to which the individual acknowledges the responsibility for his or her "plight" (i.e., internalizes or externalizes the "cause"), and/or the degree to which the depression is accompanied by anxiety, agitation, or motor excitement [conclusions, all, to which Kraeplin (1921) had come on the basis of his clinical studies]. What does not seem to get supported is the way in which depressive reactions are divided up by the Manual. That there is depression seems clear; that there are degrees of depressiveness, from neurotic to psychotic, also seems clear, but depression seems to be a much more complex phenomenon than the Manual would indicate.

CHAPTER 6

THE NEUROSES

THE APA Manual lists ten different neurotic reactions:

1. Anxiety neurosis.
2. Hysterical neurosis, conversion type.
3. Hysterical neurosis, dissociated type.
4. Phobic neurosis.
5. Obsessive-compulsive neurosis.
6. Neurasthenic neurosis.
7. Depersonalization neurosis.
8. Hypochondriacal neurosis.
9. Depressive neurosis.
10. "Other neuroses" (specific neurotic disorders not classified elsewhere, such as writer's cramp and other occupational neuroses, but does not include mixed neurosis).

On the basis of research with regard to symptoms and general behavior [e.g., Eysenck (1944), Cottle (1950), Lipman et al. (1969), Lorr and Jenkins (1953), Rao and Slater (1949), Trouton and Maxwell (1956), Williams et al. (1967, 1968)] or the data from personality questionnaires [e.g., Cattell (1933, 1943a, b, 1945a, b, 1947, 1955, 1957), Cattell and Saunders (1950), Cattell and Scheier (1961), Cattell, Dubin and Saunders (1954), Eysenck (1951, 1955a, b, 1957, 1961, 1970), Eysenck and Claridge (1962), Eysenck and Eysenck (1969), Eysenck, Eysenck and Claridge (1960), S. B. G. Eysenck (1956), Thurstone and Thurstone (1930), Winne (1951)], a general factor of neuroticism appears, one that transcends other dimensions (or traits) of personality, and one that is separate and different from a factor of psychoticism. However, other research which has focused on the same kinds of data, i.e., symptoms and behavior [e.g., Derogatis *et al.* (1970), Lorr and Rubinstein (1955, 1956), Lorr, Bishop and McNair (1965), Lorr, Rubinstein and Jenkins (1953), Lorr *et al.* (1953), McNair and Lorr (1965), O'Connor (1953) and Tatom (1958)] or questionnaire data [e.g., Mosier (1937)] does not reveal the same generalized factor of neuroticism. In this latter research, the many facets of neurotic behavior come through as factors, e.g., a sense of inadequacy, anxiety, hopelessness, etc., but absent from the resultant clusters is one definitive of neuroticism, *per se*, as in the other research. In some regard, this is an academic issue at best. For one might ask: what difference does it make if a factor of neuroticism appears or not as long as the data either cluster into syndromes which resemble the traditional neurotic subtypes or cluster into factors of symptoms and/or behavior which are traditionally associated with neuroticism rather than psychoticism? Of course, the Manual does distinguish neurotic disorders from others, and clinical theories of psychopathology also make such a differentiation, so it would be justified to expect some verification of a dimension of neuroticism, *per se*, from the data. On the other hand, the Manual groups under neuroses those subgroupings of behavior, e.g., anxiety, phobias, obsessive-compulsiveness, depression, neurasthenia, and hypochondriasis as separate neurotic conditions, whereas heretofore these have been considered aspects of more general neurotic states. (Interestingly, the Manual also includes the syndrome of depersonalization under the heading of a type of neurosis, a phenomenon ordinarily thought of to be in the borderline psychotic range of behaviors at least.) If the Manual lists these as separate entities, perhaps one should not be concerned if that is how the data turn out, and a general factor of neuroticism does not appear; from the behavioral point of view, there might not be such a factor anyway. Perhaps the fact that *some* research does not reflect a general factor of neuroticism while others do may reflect on the way in which the data of the factor analysis have been manipulated. A slightly different mode of analyzing the data (e.g. the use of rotation in one study, but not in another, or, even, of naming the factors) could account for this discrepancy.

A major question we should put to the data is: do the factors that are generated resemble the traditional diagnostic categories as outlined in the Manual or as ordinarily assumed?

Progress in answering this question is immediately impeded by a methodological issue in the research. Just in the area of the research where the basic datum is the behavior of the patient (symptom and/or general interperson behavior), of the thirteen studies to be examined closely, in only five were the subjects of the study "true" neurotics [e.g., Derogatis *et al.* (1970), Lipman *et al.* (1969), O'Connor (1953), Tatom (1958) and Williams *et al.* (1968)]. We find that the other studies in this general grouping have utilized patients from an outpatient clinic with regard to whom the only "guarantee" we have is that they are "not psychotic" [e.g., Lorr and Rubinstein (1955, 1956), Lorr, Bishop and McNair (1965), Lorr, Rubinstein and Jenkins (1953), Lorr, Schaefer, Rubinstein and Jenkins (1953), McNair and Lorr (1965)], and the patient population used in another study (Eysenck, 1944) is a group of hospitalized patients, while another (Mosier, 1937) used general college students in a class in psychology. Given that the college students are not the same as clinic patients, we might not expect a factor of neuroticism even to be evident, and one must wonder whether patients who are labelled as "not psychotic" are, *ipso facto*, neurotic. [Another hypothesis, just as tenable, is that they are individuals who have recovered from a psychotic break and are at least in partial remission, or who are in some borderline psychotic category, e.g., latent or incipient (the data will lend, I think, some support to this hypothesis).] And who is to say that patients who have to be hospitalized (regardless of the diagnosis proffered) are the same (in personality structure) as patients who do not? First, therefore, we will examine those studies wherein the subjects of the studies have been clearly identified as neurotic in the traditional sense.

O'Connor (1953) studied the symptom clustering of (over 300 V.A. male, primarily white) outpatients, all of whom had a diagnosis of one form of neurosis or another. The intercorrelation of the 120 symptoms generated seven factors:

1. Anxiety (characterized by apprehensiveness and the usual auto-nomic manifestations of anxiety).
2. Anxiety manifested primarily in physiological symptoms.
3. An obsessive-compulsive group of traits.
4. Gastro-intestinal disorders.

5. Neurasthenia (fatigue, dislike of crowds, etc.).
6. Feelings of inadequacy and inferiority.
7. A factor of hostility.

No general factor of neuroticism emerged. In some regard, however, one thinks one sees some of the neurotic reactions listed in the Manual (e.g., anxiety neurosis, hysterical neurosis, conversion type, hypochondriacal neurosis, and neurasthenic neurosis; that other "types" do not appear may simply be a function of the sample of subjects).

Tatom (1958) also utilized V.A. patients being seen in an outpatient clinic. She specifically selected for the study patients with certain diagnoses, viz., hysteria, obsessive-compulsives, anxiety state, and, for comparison, a group of non-hospitalized schizophrenics. She used a different set of data than O'Connor; whereas O'Connor stayed mainly with symptoms, Tatom focused on the broad range of behavior included in the Lorr Scale. Tatom also rotated and, hence, has produced a level of factor somewhat different than O'Connor. Nevertheless, of her unrotated factors, four emerged:

1. Unrestrained emotional behavior.
2. Maladjustment as regards social situations.
3. Passive-dependent personality.
4. A factor describing a paranoid suspiciousness and reaction to people.

The two rotated factors were:

5. A bi-polar factor, on one end describing a schizophrenic personality, on the other, a cyclothymic.
6. A factor describing uncontrolled emotionality.

As regards the unrotated factors, aside from the factor of a paranoid reaction, the other factors define characteristics found in neurotic people, but do not define the types in the Manual (as, for example, was found by O'Connor). And, moreover, no general factor of neuroticism emerges even with rotation, which, if it were a secondary factor, would bring it out.

In a series of studies, in a cooperative venture supported by NIMH, involving the analysis of responses on a symptom check list from patients from several clinics [Derogatis *et al.* (1970), Lipman *et al.* (1969), and Williams *et al.* (1968)] the data were subjected to factor analysis. The data from the three different samples generated very similar factors. In the early study by Williams *et al.* (1968), the factors generated were:

1. A general factor of neuroticism (characterized by feelings that people are unfriendly or disliked them, feelings of inferiority, feelings that others are not sympathetic or understanding of their problem, depressiveness, loneliness, feelings of being trapped, worrying, feelings of being easily hurt, temper outbursts, blaming of self, criticalness of others).
2. Anxiety manifested somatically.
3. Obsessive doubting.
4. Fearful, phobic.
5. Anxious-depressed.

In the next study (by Lipman *et al.*, 1969), the exact same factors were obtained. In the later study (Derogatis *et al.*, 1970) four factors emerged:

1. Anxiety.
2. Depression.
3. Obsessive-compulsive, phobic.
4. Hostility.

Whether the absence of the general factor of neuroticism, the clustering of phobic symptoms in the same factor with the obsessive-compulsive traits, and the introduction of a factor of hostility represents really different data or is a function of different modes of analysis, or different kinds of patient samples, cannot be discerned.

Except, therefore, for the study by Tatom, the other studies all seem to indicate that when exploring the symptom behavior of individuals diagnosed as neurotic, the clusters of symptoms that emerge do seem to be consonant with many of the types of neuroses presented in the Manual.

Some of the other research, we will see, does not lend support to this finding quite as much. Looking at the research that has been done on an unselected patient population being seen in an outpatient clinic (the studies by Lorr and his associates, and looking at them in chronological order), we find the following factors emerging from the various analyses of the behavior and symptoms of the patients:

Lorr, Rubinstein and Jenkins (1953):

1. Agitated depression.
2. Anxiety-tension.
3. Paranoid sensitivity.
4. Hostility.
5. Sexual conflicts.

Lorr *et al.* (1953): of the unrotated factors, we have:

1. Emotional lability.
2. Difficulties in adaptation to social situations.
3. A sense of personal inadequacy.
4. A lack of a sense of confidence and courage.

Of the rotated factors, we see:

5. A factor of dependence–independence.
6. Difficulty delaying the expression of impulses.
7. Degree to which a person assumes responsibility for his actions and the events that happen to him.

Lorr and Rubinstein (1955):

1. Tension (vs. relaxation).
2. Paranoid sensitivity.
3. A sense of personal inadequacy.
4. Dependence–independence.
5. Responsibility.
6. Emotional lability.
7. Gastro-intestinal reactions.
8. Cardio-respiratory reactions.
9. Sexual conflicts.
10. Psychasthenia, i.e., obsessive-compulsive traits with phobic reactions.

Two rotated factors dealt with hostility and behavior control: Lorr and Rubinstein (1956):

1. Tension–relaxation.
2. A hostile, hypersensitive, paranoid reaction to authority.
3. A sense of personal inadequacy.
4. Dependence–independence.
5. Emotional lability–stability.
6. Gastro-intestinal reactions.
7. Cardio-respiratory reactions.
8. Sexual conflicts.
9. Orderliness–indifference to order.
10. An obsessive-compulsive, phobic type, but with underlying ideas of reference.

Lorr, Bishop and McNair (1965):

1. A factor characterized by inhibitedness, submissiveness, abasiveness, an absence of dominance, competitiveness, and hostility (probably what would ordinarily be called a passive-dependent person).
2. A factor of interpersonal agreeableness, need for nurturance, affection, sociableness (or the absence of these).
3. Hostility, distrustful, detached type.
4. An exhibitionistic, dominant, competitive, and hostile type.

McNair and Lorr (1965):

1. A passive-dependent type, withdrawn and detached.
2. A passive-dependent type, but pleasant and congenial.
3. A passive-dependent type, but a person who avoids groups, but is confortable in a one-to-one relationship.
4. A friendly, congenial type (or its opposite).
5. An overtly hostile, aggressive, assertive, controlling type, seeking the attention of others, but suspicious of the motives of others, refusing help, and rarely assuming the responsibility for events of their lives.
6. An overtly hostile and aggressive type, but socially withdrawn and suspicious.

One notes some differences between the factors found in the 1965 studies by Lorr and his associates and the studies done in the fifties.

Perhaps one explanation for this is the fact that two different sets of data are used. Whereas in the studies in the fifties [except for: Lorr, Rubinstein and Jenkins (1953)], the original Lorr Scale (Lorr, 1953) data are used; the studies in the sixties employ a new scale, an Interpersonal Behavior Inventory (devised by Lorr specifically for these studies on the basis of the results of previous research on neurotics and psychoanalytic formulations). The studies where the instrument is the Interpersonal Behavior Inventory, the factors that emerge are reflective of various modes of interpersonal behavior rather than psychiatric types. The studies where the 1953 Scale is utilized, the factors that emerge resemble the more traditional psychiatric types, or reflect personality factors associated with neuroticism. Undoubtedly, the kinds of behavior being rated introduce differences in the factors that emerge.

Probably, to some extent, with patients similar to that used by Lorr *et al.* is that found in the study by Eysenck (1944). Having studied veterans who were labeled as with "reactive types of mental illness", generally carrying a diagnosis of some form of neurosis, but who were hospitalized for treatment, Eysenck found the following four factors:

1. A general factor of neuroticism.
2. A bi-polar factor characterized, at one end, by psychasthenia (symptoms of obsessive-compulsiveness, depression, irritability) vs. hysteria (somatic complaints, sexual anomalies, neurasthenic, lacking group membership, unskilled).
3. Neurasthenia (hypochondriasis, dyspepsia, low energy, somatic anxiety).
4. A bi-polar factor with characteristics of a schizoid personality at one end and a cyclical personality at the other.

One could, of course, "argue" with the labels Eysenck may give to his factors. For example, that which he calls "hysteric" (involving somatic complaints, sexual anomalies, neurasthenic, lacking group membership, and unskilled) might not find popular agreement amongst clinicians. And his factor of neuroticism (characterized by: "badly organized personality", dependence, symptoms of pathology evident even before the necessity for hospitalization, narrow life interests, low energy, dyspepsia, schizoid personality, poor muscle tonus, no group membership, cycloid or schizoid personality type, a history of unemployment, unsatisfactory home life, abnormalities in parents, and having been discharged from service because of their psychological difficulties) might better have been termed a factor of psychopathology, *per se*. However, a general factor of neuroticism does emerge; the traditional differentiation of neurosis into the obsessive-compulsive and hysteric types appears, as does a neurasthenic type. The schizoid-cyclical factor may or may not reflect a more-than-just-neurotic type of patient having been used in the study, or this dimension may be tapping in to the introvert–extravert dimension, though not so named.

The final study we shall explore was the one done by Mosier (1937). He gave the Thurstone Neurotic Inventory to college students, and whereas Thurstone (Thurstone and Thurstone, 1930), in using this Inventory, *had* found an overall factor of neuroticism emerging from the factor analysis, Mosier did not. Instead of finding the general factor, or, even, the more traditional neurotic types (e.g., obsessive-compulsive or hysteric), he found types characterized by:

1. Cycloid tendency (experiencing mood swings, unhappiness, grouchiness, difficulty making up one's mind).
2. Depressiveness (periods of loneliness, low spirits, unhappiness, difficulty making friends).
3. Hypersensitivity (feelings easily hurt, cannot stand criticism, easily discouraged).
4. Lack of self-confidence.
5. Social introversion (shy, retreats in social situations, feelings of inferiority, lacking self-confidence, hypersensitive to what people are thinking about them).
6. Self-consciousness (difficulty speaking in public, stage fright, self-conscious reciting, hesitant to volunteer in class).
7. Depressed re scholastic performance.
8. Autistic tendency (frequent daydreams, periods of loneliness, burdened by a sense of remorse, self-conscious about personal appearance, obsessive, feelings of loneliness even when in the company of others, feelings of being watched on the street).

It is tempting to interpret the difference between the studies by Mosier and Thurstone as being due to the samples of subjects each used; that what comes through in Mosier's data are psychological *problems* without there being a factor of neuroticism because the group was not composed of neurotics, *per se.*

Turning to test data, we find that on the basis of a variety of non-projective tests, Foulds [e.g., Foulds (1959, 1961, 1962, 1965), Foulds and Caine (1958, 1959)] and Lubin (1970) were able to differentiate what appeared to be hysterics from obsessive-compulsives. No general factor of neuroticism or of other neurotic types appeared. As regards the Wechsler scales, we note that both Wechsler (1944) and Rapaport (Rapaport, Gill and Schafer, 1945) had some rather specific notions about the performance of neurotics, particularly in terms of the patterning of the subtests, which have not been supported by research [e.g., Dana (1957), Gilhooly (1950), Heyer (1949), Lewinski (1945), Warner (1950)]. What does receive support is the *qualitative* aspects of the performance of the neurotics on the Wechsler. For example, the very anxious person may have difficulty attending and concentrating or remembering (revealing difficulty with digits, arithmetic, or digit symbol, but also commenting, showing concern about inadequate performance), or the intellectualizing stiltedness of the obsessive will be reflected in verbalizations (i.e., on vocabulary, similarities, comprehension, etc., anywhere where an explanation is called for). Clearly, the qualitative aspect of the performance of the neurotic on the Wechsler scales will not reflect the thought disorder of the schizophrenic nor the perceptual distortion or alienation from reality of the psychotic.

The findings with regard to the neurotic's performance on the Wechsler seem replicated with regard to the Rorschach. For all of the clinical assumptions regarding the neurotic's response, for example, to color (e.g., color shock or responses where form is not predominant in determining the response but the color is), or content (e.g., that animal percepts would predominate as compared to humans), the studies [e.g., Fisher (1951), Goldfarb (1943), Harrower-Erickson (1942), Lyle (1956), Miale and Harrower-Erickson (1940), Reitzell (1949)] do not reveal any unique pattern of performance for neurotics with regard to *any* of the formal elements of the Rorschach or the Rorschach as a task. Again, as with the Wechsler, the obsessiveness of the obsessive comes through qualitatively, as does the anxiety of the generally anxious and/or phobic person.

When we turn to the MMPI, we find that the bulk of the data point in favor of a clearcut differentiation between the neurotic and the psychotic [e.g., Dahlstrom and Prange (1960), Gough (1946), Guthrie (1950), Meehl (1946), Meehl and Dahlstrom (1960), Rosen (1962), Rubin (1948), Silver and Sines (1961), Wheeler *et al.* (1951), Winne (1951)], both as regards the absence of signs of psychosis with the neurotics (e.g., on the Schizophrenia and Ego Strength Scales), as well as what has come to be known as the neurotic triad, viz., elevated performance on the Hysteria, Depression, and Hypochondriases Scales [e.g., Dahlstrom and Prange (1960), Gough (1946), Guthrie (1950), McKinley and Hathaway (1940, 1942, 1944), Wheeler *et al.* (1951)]. However, it is also incumbent upon us to note that both Schmidt (1945) and Morris (1947) found, as regards their data, that although all psychopathological groups could be differentiated from non-psychiatric controls, they could not be differentiated, one from the other. In their data, 24% of the time, the neurotic is labeled psychotic by the MMPI and 29% of the time, the psychotic is labeled neurotic (Meehl, 1946). Schmidt and Morris did not find that their data permitted a refined discrimination between the hysteric, the obsessive, or the hypochondriac.[5]

What can we, now, say regarding the neuroses and the attempt to validate the types as outlined in the Manual? In the first place, we can see that in general, in terms of behavioral and test data, there is support for the psychiatric differentiation between neurosis and psychosis, as made traditionally, and as outlined in the Manual. In some of the research, particularly that which focuses on behavior, the general factor of neuroticism does not come through, and, moreover, the data reflect psychological *problems* rather than psychiatric types. The former can easily be accounted for in terms of the method of analysis of the data (i.e., the manner of factoring, when simple structure is presumed, and whether rotation is performed or not); the presence or absence of such a factor could be a function of the statistical method used by the

[5] Perhaps part of the difficulty in making refined discriminations with the MMPI is in the instrument itself. In several studies where he has factor analyzed the data gleaned from the specific scales, Comrey (1957a, b, c, 1958a, b, c) has demonstrated that, for example, the Hypochondriasis, Depression, Hysteria, Hypomania and Psychasthenia Scales are not unidimensional. They all are composed of several factors, only one of which has to do with the specific psychopathology identified by the Scale. This reduces the specificity of the Scales and, hence, the possibility of finding results uniquely specific to one or another group.

investigator to extract the meaning from the data. Both consequences (i.e., the presence or absence of a general factor of neuroticism and the presence of factors reflective of basic psychological problems, e.g., personal and/or social inadequacy, degree of hostility, presence of sexual conflicts, dependence–independence, degree and quality of control over feelings and impulses, etc.) can easily be accounted for in terms of the nature of the input in the research. Different kinds of data (i.e., interpersonal vs. psychiatric) yield, obviously, different factors.

As regards the neurotic types presented in the Manual, both behavioral and test data seem to point to a clearcut differentiation between (and, hence, support the individual representation of) obsessive-compulsive neurosis and hysteria, thus validating the existence of these two types as delineated in the Manual. Moreover, some of the research on current behavior (interpersonal and psychiatric) of the neurotic validates the presence of separate entities of such neurotic reactions (types) as: anxiety state, phobias, neurasthenia, and depression, much as is outlined in the Manual. Sometimes the phobic reaction clusters with the obsessive-compulsive, much in the manner of Kraeplin's concept of psychasthenia, and we see more the presence of somatizers, rather than a clearcut differentiation into hysterical neuroses, conversion type and hypochondriacal neurosis. Not supported by the research was the presence of: hysterical neurosis (dissociative type), depersonalization neurosis, or occupational neuroses, as presented in the Manual. Sometimes a factor of paranoid sensitivity or schizoidness appears in the data on the neurotics, but that would seem to be a function of the samples utilized (i.e., hospitalized or non-specific outpatient groups who are assumed to be neurotic simply because they are not manifestly psychotic).

Many problems attend the concept of neurosis. In the first place, although William Cullen introduced the term "neurosis" in 1769 (Knoff, 1970), the term has yet to be clarified: does it mean: symptoms, the syndrome, or the basic personality, and does it simply mean the absence of psychosis? Moreover, there does not appear to be such a thing as *a* neurosis, rather, there appears to be degrees of neurotic involvement and varying degrees of severity (Chapman and Chapman, 1967) within the various subtypes, a dimension that transcends type, which make clearcut differentiation, descriptively or prognostically, difficult. There are people whose symptoms of their neurosis are somatic and some non-somatic (i.e., ideational or affective) (Downing and Rickels, 1965), and even within the somatic realm, the situation is quite complex. For example, Comrey (1957a) found that somatic difficulties of the neurotic factored out into parameters of: poor physical health, digestive difficulties, visual difficulties, lung difficulty, bowel dysfunction, sinusitis, or general hypochondriasis. O'Connor and Stefic (1959) found clusterings (from MMPI data) re: neurasthenia, vague somatic complaints, G-I reactions, and poor physical health. Obviously, even such a dimension as somatizers, with regard to neurosis, subsumes a variety of styles; why should we expect that they should be similar either as regards the underlying psychopathology or general personality type merely because they share the same manifestation of, let us say, anxiety or neurotic reaction expressed somatically?

Another factor in reducing the degree of homogeneity and, hence, clarity with regard to samples of neurotics even sharing the same label as it were is that not only do we have to differentiate the person with an obsessive-compulsive neurosis from an obsessive-compulsive character, as well as degrees of obsessionality, but we must also be careful to note when obsessive symptoms mask an underlying psychosis (Freud, 1913) or where the obsessive or compulsive traits assume psychotic proportions (i.e., obsessive-compulsive psychosis, a term rarely used any more in psychiatry). Moreover, factor analysis of behavior data reveals that the obsessive-compulsive neurosis is really made up of *two* major syndromes, viz., the obsessive *and* the compulsive (Sandler and Hazari, 1960), and that an analysis of case history data (e.g., Lewis, 1936) suggests an even different kind of dichotomy, viz., an obstinate, morose, irritable person and a vacillating, uncertain, submissive person.

The same kind of comments obtain with regard to hysteria. The assumption of some simple truth to the diagnostic entity is, on closer scrutiny, seen to be simplistic. As a diagnostic entity, hysteria does seem to exist (e.g., Wittenborn and Holzberg, 1951a), but the diagnosis seems to cover a multitude of traits [e.g., Chodoff and Lyons (1958), Easser and Lesser (1965), Mallet and Gold (1964), Noble (1951)]. In these studies, it is found that the term hysteria is used to describe:

1. The pattern of behavior habitually exhibited by certain individuals who are said to be hysterical personalities (which, of course, is tautological).
2. A particular kind of psychosomatic symptom cluster i.e., conversion reactions.
3. A disorder characterized by phobia and/or free-floating anxiety (i.e., anxiety hysteria).
4. A personality whose major defence is repression.
5. A personality characterized by the presence of fugue states.
6. A term of approbium.
7. That hysteria has many facets: dysfunction of an organ, fear of sexuality, pansexuality, *belle indifférence*, suggestibility, manipulativeness (Wisdom, 1961); poor physical health, shyness, cynicism, headaches (Comrey, 1957c).
8. That hysteria should be differentiated in terms of reference to symptoms and to character [e.g., Foulds (1964), Ingham and Robinson (1964)].
9. That conversion reactions are considered as: defense against anxiety, as transmuted energy, as a symbolic communication, as the mental being expressed organically (Ziegler and Imboden, 1962).
10. That hysterical symptoms of any kind can exist in a variety of psychiatric states, not just hysteria [e.g., Chodoff and Lyons (1958), Rangell (1959), Slater (1961)].
11. That not every psychosomatic illness is to be considered a conversion reaction (Rangell, 1959).
12. That hysteria exists within the whole gamut of reactions defined by the continuum of ego strength (and weakness) [e.g., Marmor (1953), Noble (1951), Zetzel (1968)], to the point of hysterical symptoms being able to be present as a basic personality type, in a formal neurosis, or even in a psychotic state [though not popular, psychiatric terminology contains reference to the concept of hysterical psychosis, e.g., Hirsch and Hollender (1969), Hollender and Hirsch (1964), Lazare (1971), Mallet and Gold (1964), Noble (1951), Somopoulos (1971)].

What can we, now, say about neurosis? By and large, test data (particularly the Rorschach and the Wechsler) reflect basic traits or issues, but not types; support for the psychiatric types, as outlined in the Manual, seems to come primarily from behavioral data. However, even here, a more intensive exploration of the data reveals that what has, heretofore, been subsumed under a single diagnostic label, e.g., obsessive-compulsive, hysteric, somatic reaction, etc., turns out to be, rather, a complex variety of individuals. The diagnostic terms, therefore, appear to obscure more than they reveal.

CHAPTER 7

OUTCOME

THUS far we have seen that the information consistently relatable to diagnoses is current symptom behavior. We have also seen that life history events and the psychological functions assessed by psychological tests such as the Rorschach and the Wechsler, do not relate in any consistent way to diagnoses. Having looked backwards, to the patient's past, and intensively at the patient's present, we should, now, turn our attention to the future time perspective. As Jenkins (1953) has noted, as far back as the time of Hippocrates, an adequate diagnosis was felt to be necessary in order to plan for treatment. One can find this sentiment reflected in the ideas of many current workers in the field of psychopathology, e.g., Astrup *et al.* (1962), Bullard (1960), Cameron (1953), Caverny *et al.* (1955), Cohen (1943), Cole (1965), Fairweather *et al.* (1960), Fiske (1956), Gesell *et al.* (1919), Hunt (1951), Hunt, Wittson and Hunt (1953), Kahn (1969), Katz *et al.* (1965), Lorr (1953b), Sarbin (1944), Stone and Skurdal (1968), Thorne (1945, 1953, 1964) and Watson (1951a, b). Even Freud subscribed to that notion:

> "... the whole value of ... nosographical distinctions, one which quite justifies them, lies in the fact that they indicate a different aetiology and a different therapy" (Freud, 1910, p. 301).

Of course, not every clinician believes as strongly in the communicative value of diagnostic statements; Adolf Meyer (1917) did not believe that these statements *should* have predictive value, that is, be expected to; Carl Rogers agrees, commenting that behavior is lawful (i.e., dependable), but not predictable.

Reviewing the research in this area, we see that the weight of evidence

57

is that specific psychiatric diagnosis is not useful as regards prediction in general,[6] or in response to specific forms of psychiatric treatment, e.g., carbon dioxide inhalation (Moriarty, 1954; Smith, 1952), drugs (Klein, 1967), lobotomy (Jackson and Jaco, 1954), or the coma-inducing therapies such as with metrazol,[7] insulin,[8] or electric shock.[9] The same generally negative finding has been true as regards specific symptoms as well [e.g., Albee (1951), Dawson and Weingold (1966), Lanzkron and Wolfson (1958), Stone (1969)]. The best we seem able to say is that, for example, the diagnosis of schizophrenia, *per se*, generally carries with it a poor prognosis [e.g., Fuller (1930), Fuller and Johnston (1931a), Lehrman (1960), Mason *et al.* (1960), Pascal *et al.* (1953), Silverman (1941)]. Indeed, prognosis seems better estimated by factors *other* than the diagnosis, e.g., degree of psychopathology [e.g., Cancro (1969), Ellsworth and Clayton (1959), Eskey and Friedman (1958), Eskey *et al.* (1957), Hiler (1966), Kant (1944), Lindemann *et al.* (1959), McKeever and May (1964)], personality characteristics [e.g., Kahn and Fink (1959), Levine and Wittenborn (1970)], the relative shortness of the duration of the serious phase of the disturbance (so-called; acute

---

[6] E.g., Arthur and Gunderson (1966a, b), Bannister *et al.* (1964), Brown and Kosterlitz (1964), Clow (1953), Feldman *et al.* (1954), Fuller (1930), Fulton and Lorei (1967), Gunderson and Arthur (1968), Hunt and Appell (1936), Kant (1940, 1941a, b), Lewinsohn (1967), Lindemann *et al.* (1959), Linn (1962), Mason *et al.* (1960), Masterson (1956, 1958), Phillips and Zigler (1964), Rennie (1943), Roman and Ebaugh (1938), Rupp and Fletcher (1940), Schofield *et al.* (1954), Silverman (1941), Swensen and Pascal (1954a, b).

[7] E.g., Beckenstein (1939), Bianchi and Chiarello (1944), Bowman *et al.* (1939), Chase and Silverman (1943), Cheney and Drewry (1938), Kolb and Vogel (1942), Lipschutz *et al.* (1939), Low *et al.* (1938), Notkin *et al.* (1940), Pacella and Barrera (1943), Pollock (1939), Read *et al.* (1939), Reznikoff (1940), Williams *et al.* (1939), Wilson (1939), Zeifert (1941), Ziskind *et al.* (1942).

[8] E.g., Bond (1941), Bond and Rivers (1942, 1944), Bowman *et al.* (1939), Chase and Silverman (1943), Cheney and Clow (1941), Cheney and Drewry (1938), Katzenbogen *et al.* (1939), Kolb and Vogel (1942), Lipschutz *et al.* (1939), Malzberg (1938, 1939), Miller (1939), Niver *et al.* (1939), Notkin *et al.* (1939), Palmer *et al.* (1950), Polatin and Spotnitz (1943), Ross and Malzberg (1939), Ross *et al.* (1941), Salzman (1947), Strecker (1938), Taylor and Von Salzen (1938), Whitehead (1937).

[9] E.g., Alexander (1945), Bianchi and Chiarello (1944), Brill *et al.* (1959), Epstein (1943), Gold and Chiarello (1944), Gralnick (1946), Hamilton (1947), Hemphill and Walter (1941), Herzberg (1954), Kalinowsky and Barrera (1940), Kalinowsky and Worthing (1943), Kalinowsky *et al.* (1941), Kolb and Vogel (1942), Malzberg (1943), Neymann *et al.* (1943), Pacella and Barrera (1943), Rennie (1943), Reznikoff (1943), Smith *et al.* (1942, 1943).

onset)[10] (duration of less than six months of the acute phase before treatment was found to lead to a good prognosis to *any* form of psychiatric treatment *regardless* of diagnosis including schizophrenia). Indeed, Masserman (Masserman and Carmichael, 1938) demonstrated that prognosis is an event predicated on a multiplicity of factors, viz.,

1. Constitutional make-up (both physical as well as mental).
2. The nature and intensity of previous psychotic or neurotic reactions.
3. The results of therapy attempted previously.
4. The duration, type, and severity of the presenting illness.
5. Depth and plasticity of emotional conflicts and maladjustments with regard to reality.
6. The degree of rapport that could be obtained currently.
7. The amount of insight that could be generated in even the superficial clinical contacts.

But most interestingly, as it turns out, one of the best predictors of behavior is behavior, viz., the patient's behavior in the hospital turns out to be the best predictor of length of hospitalization and response to treatment [e.g., Fairweather *et al.* (1956), Mendel (1966), Nuttall and Solomon (1965, 1970), Simmons and Tyler (1969)]. Predictions of outcome were found to be better made from the date from behavioral inventories, therefore, than from formal diagnosis [e.g., from the Lorr Scale (Goldberg *et al.*, 1967; Klett and Mosley, 1965) or the Hospital Adjustment Scale (e.g., Ferguson *et al.*, 1953)].

Probably *the* most telling criticism of psychiatric diagnosis is that it

---

[10] E.g., Aldrich and Coffin (1948), Aldrich *et al.* (1949), Beckenstein (1939), Bianchi and Chiarello (1944), Boisen (1933), Chapman *et al.* (1961), Danziger and Kindwall (1946), Ellsworth and Clayton (1959), Farina *et al.* (1962, 1963), Fulton and Lorei (1967), Gold and Chiarello (1944), Gonda (1941), Hunt *et al.* (1938), Jenkins and Gurel (1959), Kalinowsky and Worthing (1943), Kalinowsky *et al.* (1941), Kant (1940a, b, 1941b), Lewis and Blanchard (1931), Libertson (1941), Linn (1962), Low *et al.* (1938), Malamud and Render (1939), Malzberg (1938), Masterson (1958), McKendree (1942), Nameche *et al.* (1964), Nielson *et al.* (1942), Notkin *et al.* (1940), Nuttall and Solomon (1965), Pollock (1939), Reznikoff (1940, 1943), Rupp and Fletcher (1940), Schofield *et al.* (1954), Silverman (1941), Simon and Wirt (1961), Steen (1933), Stephens *et al.* (1966), Strecker (1938), Vaillant (1962, 1963, 1964), Walker and Kelley (1960), Wanklin *et al.* (1956), Whitehead (1937, 1938), Wittman (1948), Zeifert (1941).

is not the stuff out of which decisions regarding treatability by psychotherapy is made, either in general [e.g., Bannister *et al.* (1964), Garfield and Affleck (1959, 1961), Meehl (1960), Patterson (1948), Rogers (1946), Slavson (1950), Snygg and Combs (1949), Weinstock (1965), Wolstein (1964)], or in terms of such specific forms of psychotherapy as psychoanalysis [e.g., Fine (1968, 1970), Freud (1910, 1913), Guttman (1960), Knapp *et al.* (1960), Namnum (1968)] or behavior therapy [e.g., Goldfriend and Pomeranz (1968)].[11] Some research [e.g., by Harrower (1970)] suggests that the prediction of whether the patient will stay in treatment or degree of improvement from psychotherapy can be made from psychological test data, but, again, the predictions are made from the traditional psychological dimensions of personality rather than psychiatric. The "cruelest" blow of all seems to be that psychiatric diagnosis does not even seem to relate to whether the patient should be hospitalized or not (!) [e.g., Mendel and Rapport (1969)].

What the studies do seem to show, with minor exception, is that the outcome of any form of psychiatric treatment is not a function of the particular diagnosis; indeed, this seems to be virtually irrelevant. *The dimension that seems to emerge from the many studies as being able to predict whether individuals will respond well to psychiatric treatment is pre-morbid adjustment.* From the earliest days in modern psychiatry, it was clear that there was a dichotomous dimension in schizophrenia, for example, that cut across the traditional diagnostic categories. It must be remembered that Kraeplin (1902) recognized that there was a group of patients diagnosed as dementia praecox who did not conform to his notions of the kind of premorbid personality and outcome characteristics of dementia praecox, i.e., their background did not reflect what was ultimately to be called the "shut in" or, later, schizoid personality from which Kraeplin believed dementia praecox to develop, and their course of illness was not in the direction of increasing deterioration. Bleuler (1950) made the same observation, referring to them differentially as "schizophrenia" and "schizophreniform" psychoses. Adolf Meyer (1903) noted the same distinction, referring to the good

---

[11] I am not sure what to do with this datum, but Meehl (1960) seems to feel that only 17% of clinicians believe that *any* knowledge of the patient's personality has *anything* to do with the progress of psychotherapy.

and poor nature of their premorbid life. He was aware of the differential prognosis from these differing backgrounds, as were such clinical investigators as Williams and Potter (1921), Levin (1931), Lewis and Blanchard (1931), Boisen (1933), Hunt and Appell (1936), Kasanin (1933), Steen (1933), etc. Kasanin (Kasanin and Kaufman, 1929) was cognizant of their good and premorbid history in general, but chose to focus on the fact that some patients were clearly reacting to stress, while the "stress" for others did not seem, from the outside observer, to be really stressful. He, therefore, differentiated these two kinds of patients as "nuclear" and "reactive". It would appear that Langfeldt (1937) formulated this notion into what has come to be called the process–reactive dimension within schizophrenia. Recall that the same differentiation was found as regards depression.[12] This parameter of process–reaction in psychiatric illness has proven to be the more relevant dimension correlating with outcome of psychiatric treatment, as regards hospitalization and the general progress of psychiatric disorders over time[13]

---

[12] On pp. 46–47.

[13] E.g., Adler (1953), Aldrich and Coffin (1948), Aldrich *et al.* (1949), Arthur and Gunderson (1966a, b), Astrup *et al.* (1962), Bannister *et al.* (1964), Bayard and Pascal (1954), Boisen (1933), Bond and Braceland (1937), Brown and Kosterlitz (1964), Cameron (1955), Cancro (1969), Cancro and Sugerman (1968), Chapman *et al.* (1961), Chase and Silverman (1943), Clow (1953), Clum and Hoiberg (1971), Cole *et al.* (1954), Counts and Devlin (1954), Danziger and Kindwall (1946), Davis *et al.* (1971), Dunham and Meltzer (1946), Ellsworth and Clayton (1969), Eskey and Friedman (1958), Farina and Webb (1956), Farina *et al.* (1962, 1963), Feldman *et al.* (1954), Fuller and Johnston (1931a, b), Fulton and Lorei (1967), Garfield and Sundland (1966), Garmezy (1965), Gittelman-Klein and Klein (1968), Gold and Chiarello (1944), Gonda (1941), Gundersen and Arthur (1968), Harrow *et al.* (1969), Hunt and Appell (1936), Hunt *et al.* (1938), Jenkins and Gurel (1959), Johannsen *et al.* (1963), Jones *et al.* (1965), Kalinowsky and Worthing (1943), Kalinowsky *et al.* (1941), Kant (1940a, 1941a, b), Kasanin (1933), Langfeldt (1953, 1959), Levin (1931), Lewis and Blanchard (1931), Libertson (1941), Lindemann *et al.* (1959), Linn (1962), Low (1938), Malamud and Malamud (1943), Malamud and Render (1939), Malzberg (1938), Marks *et al.* (1963), Mason *et al.* (1960), Masterson (1956, 1958), McKendree (1942), Michaels (1959), Moran *et al.* (1955), Nameche *et al.* (1964), Nielsen *et al.* (1942), Notkin *et al.* (1939, 1940), Nuttall and Solomon (1965, 1970), Orr *et al.* (1955), Pascal *et al.* (1953), Phillips (1953), Phillips and Zigler (1964), Pokorny (1962), Pollock (1939), Query and Query (1964), Rennie (1942, 1943), Reznikoff (1940, 1943), Rivers and Bond (1941), Romano and Ebaugh (1938), Rosen *et al.* (1968, 1969, 1971), Rupp and Fletcher (1940), Schofield *et al.* (1954), Shader *et al.* (1967), Silverman (1941), Simon and Wirt (1961), Steen (1933), Stephens and Astrup (1963), Stephens *et al.* (1966, 1967, 1969), Strecker (1938), Swensen and

or response to carbon dioxide inhalation,[14] drugs,[15] lobotomy,[16] ECT,[17] insulin,[18] or metrazol[19] treatment, in particular.

Pascal (1954a, b), Vaillant (1962, 1963, 1964), Walker and Kelley (1960), Wanklin *et al.* (1956), Whitehead (1937, 1938), Wittman (1941, 1948), Wittman and Steinberg (1944), Zeifert (1941), Zigler and Phillips (1960, 1961a, b, c, 1962).

[14] E.g., Moriarty (1954), Smith (1952).

[15] E.g., Klein (1967).

[16] E.g., Jackson and Jaco (1954).

[17] E.g., Bianchi and Chiarello (1944), Bowman *et al.* (1939), Chase and Silverman (1943), Cheney and Drewry (1938), Danziger and Kindwall (1946), Gold and Chiarello (1944), Gonda (1941), Kalinowsky and Worthing (1943), Kalinowsky *et al.* (1941), Katzenbogen *et al.* (1939), Kolb and Vogel (1942), Libertson (1941), Lipschutz *et al.* (1939), Low *et al.* (1938), Malzberg (1943), Notkin *et al.* (1940), Pacella and Barrera (1940), Pollock (1939), Read *et al.* (1939), Reznikoff (1940, 1943), Williams *et al.* (1939), Wilson (1939), Zeifert (1941), Ziskind *et al.* (1942).

[18] E.g., Bond (1941), Bond and Rivers (1942, 1944), Bowman *et al.* (1939), Chase and Silverman (1943), Cheney and Clow (1941), Cheney and Drewry (1938), Katzenbogen *et al.* (1939), Kolb and Vogel (1942), Lipschutz *et al.* (1939), Malzberg (1938, 1939), McKendree (1942), Miller (1939), Nielsen *et al.* (1942), Niver *et al.* (1939), Notkin *et al.* (1939), Palmer *et al.* (1950), Polatin and Spotnitz (1943), Rivers and Bond (1941), Ross and Malzberg (1939), Ross *et al.* (1941), Salzman (1947), Strecker (1938), Taylor and Von Salzen (1938), Whitehead (1937).

[19] E.g., Beckenstein (1939), Bianchi and Chiarello (1944), Bowman *et al.* (1939), Chase and Silverman (1943), Cheney and Drewry (1938), Kolb and Vogel (1942), Lipschutz *et al.* (1939), Low *et al.* (1938), Notkin *et al.* (1940), Pacella and Barrera (1940), Pollock (1939), Read *et al.* (1939), Reznikoff (1940), Williams *et al.* (1939), Wilson (1939), Zeifert (1941), Ziskind *et al.* (1942).

CHAPTER 8

BEYOND THE DIAGNOSTIC PRINCIPLE

To diagnose, or not to diagnose, that is the question; whether 'tis nobler to suffer the slings and arrows of an outrageous system of classification, or to take arms against this sea of troubles, and by opposing, end them . . .

We have asked ourselves a question regarding the usefulness of psychiatric diagnosis. We translated that question into a somewhat more specific form—what information is tendered by psychiatric diagnoses? and we looked for the answer to this question to the patient's behavior, past, present, and future. From a review of the research we have learned that different kinds of data focus on different facets of behavior. Thus, behavior viewed directly, as in an interview or through observation, yields information regarding the patient's symptoms. Behavior as recorded in the patient's case history generates information regarding his or her *social* behavior, and behavior elicited by psychological tests yields information about cognitive functions and the degree of presence of certain psychological conflicts and problems as well as traits.[20] Moreover, the data indicate that there does not seem to be any consistent relationship amongst the patterns of these various segments of personality.[21] The second major conclusion that might be drawn from

[20] This is an apparent confirmation of Saul Rosenzweig's insight that different techniques in clinical work tap different levels and facets of personality (Rosenzweig, 1950).

[21] Though Vernis (1968) found that the data from inventories were as effective in assessing the general level of the patients' difficulties as were interviews, Calhoun (1971) found a correlation of 0.447 between the data from interview and behavioral observations, and Harris *et al.* (1970) found correlations between observed data (via behavioral scales) and interview of 0.24 for suspiciousness, and 0.40 for paranoia; Abrams *et al.* (1966) found a 0.30 correlation between rating of paranoia from interview vs. the Paranoia Scale of the MMPI, and Grant *et al.* (1952) found that judgments of adjustment made from interview do not match that made from Rorschach protocols.

these data is that only behavior as viewed directly, as in interview, i.e., current, manifest symptoms, cluster with any consistency to and match, to any degree, the groupings found in the system of classification of psychopathology as presented in the Manual. Psychiatric diagnoses, therefore, prove to be a purely descriptive system of classification, yielding no useful information regarding the life of the individual (beyond the observable in the present, i.e., his symptoms), the prognosis for the person's rehabilitation, or what methods would best be suited to facilitate that rehabilitation. Moreover, though syndromes (i.e., groupings of symptoms) *do* emerge from these data, few symptoms prove to be syndrome (i.e., diagnosis) specific. This confirms the same observation made by Kraeplin (1902) on the basis of his clinical studies. With minor exception, as, for example, the thought disorder of the schizophrenic which seems unique to the individual identified as a schizophrenic, syndromes seem to entail configurations based on vir- tually a finite set of behaviors. Hence, we may conclude that all person- alities seem to be a function of (composite of) some basic behavioral dimensions, with the difference between one person and another seeming to be the pattern of the relationship of these dimensions. This certainly seems to confirm Eysenck's comment (Eysenck, 1955b) that personality is a multidimensional event, with the personality of any one individual defined by the position of that individual in a multidimen- sional psychological space. Finally, granted the general confirmation of the psychiatric system of classification as presented in the Manual in terms of symptom behavior, taken individually or in groups, symptoms do not reveal any significant relationship to outcome of any form of treatment, or life history events. At the start we noted that there were classification systems that were exclusively descriptive, while others provided additional information as regards function. We also noted that for some data, a purely descriptive system was adequate, but that with regard to those phenomena that are capable of some action, the system of classification must include that dimension in its context. Humans live, not just manifest behavior. A system of classification of behavior which has little relevance to the life of the individual, past, present, or future, seems hardly adequate.

In evaluation of any research, one should inquire as to the possible reasons why an hypothesis was not supported. It is, of course, possible that the hypothesis is simply not tenable. It might also be that the way the hypothesis was tested, the structure of the study, precluded a favorable test of the hypothesis. Therefore, let us look at some aspects of the design of this research, aspects which might have mitigated against a more favorable support of the hypothesis that psychiatric diagnoses are meaningful and useful statements.

First in our consideration is the nature of the data itself. Human behavior is so complex that very often its meaning is defined by the context. Thus, the behavior of the person in his home environ, on a ward, or in a clinician's office, might very much be a function of the situation, or at least reflect some of the stimulus and/or demand characteristics of the situation. That, in and of itself, could interfere with (indeed, if not preclude) being able to find consistency for a person from one social context in his life to another. This might explain the lack of concordance between the behavior of the present (i.e., symptoms) with the past (i.e., life history) or the future. On the other hand, there was sufficient randomness in the behavior as recorded in the external environment, the environment of the ward, and the reaction to a variety of treatment modalities, in and of themselves, that consistency did not seem to be the characteristic of these data even when looking at the relationship of one set of data by itself to diagnosis. Second, because of the complexity of behavior, sometimes it is just too difficult to assign a set of behaviors to a single category.[22] Third: we must contend with the ambiguity inherent in the terms themselves. For example, we note that although the term "neurosis" was introduced into psychiatric parlance at least as early as the mid-eighteenth century [Bowman and Rose (1951), Knoff (1970)], and the term "psychosis" was introduced in the mid-nineteenth century [Diethelm (1953)], there is still no consensus as to the meaning of the terms. To some, psychosis means alienation and withdrawal from reality; to some, it means being the victim, as it were, of fantasies which, now, have become conscious; to some, it has developmental implications; to some, it simply means alien from the mainstream of ordinary behavior. Similarly, the diagnosis of neurosis is frequently made as a signification of the absence of mani-

[22] E.g., Hunt and Walker (1962), Hunt, Schwartz and Walker (1965), Hunt, Wittson and Hunt (1952, 1955), Kostlan (1954), Pumroy and Kogan (1955), Sandifer et al. (1964), Schmidt and Fonda (1956).

festations of psychosis, behavioral or defense; i.e., a diagnosis by exclusion. Fourth: is the way clinicians assign diagnostic labels in difficult-to-diagnose cases. It has been found that if the clinician does not truly understand the patient's condition, and if the behavior is in the psychotic range, the probability is that the person will be diagnosed as a schizophrenic (Kahn and Pokorny, 1964); if it is in the neurotic range, the patient will probably be diagnosed as an hysteric (Slater, 1961).

We should also focus on the research methodology. For example, in his analysis of the situation, Comrey (1962) noted that the following methodological issues could influence the research findings in terms of biasing or distorting the results:

1. The kinds of samples studied.
2. The size of the samples.
3. The type of the item used to explore behavior.
4. The factor complexity of the items.
5. The size of the correlation.
6. The size of the correlation matrix to be analyzed.
7. The method of correlation used.
8. The method of factor extraction (if factor analysis is employed).
9. When simple structure is decided upon in analyzing the factor matrix.
10. Hence the number of factors extracted, and
11. Whether rotation is performed, and if so,
12. The method of rotation used.

To this, we can add that the nature of the instrument used to gather the data might account for some degree of variation (i.e., inconsistency) in the results of the various studies. For example, although several investigators might be approaching the phenomena of psychopathology from a purely behavioral point of view, and both are employing behavioral inventories from which to record such data, different inventories, not focusing on the same facets of behavior, will introduce variation in the results. Moreover, even if the approach is behavioral, but one investigator's data are derived from observations made on the ward, while another's are from interview data, that, in and of itself, will produce different results. Another aspect of the research methodology that deserves consideration, in part, as Comrey pointed out, is the method of analyzing the data. Behavior is too complex to be explored via a correlational technique which compares one set of data with another. Spitzer [e.g., Overall and Hollister (1964), Spitzer and Endicott (1968), Spitzer et al. (1964)], amongst others, has suggested the use of computers to encompass the complexity of the data, and, stemming from the seminal work of Spearman (1929), factor analysis has, now, been used for some time by the more sophisticated researchers. Comrey (1962), Lorr (1957) and Wittenborn (1964) have demonstrated that if you just analyze the same data by a different method, different results eventuate.

Finally, another aspect of the research methodology which should receive our critical attention is the parameter of the rater. We already know from other research in clinical and social psychology [e.g., Bieri et al. (1966)] that judgments made by raters may differ significantly by virtue of their own personal frames of reference; why should we not expect that this factor might not be an important dimension in influencing the results of the studies we are reviewing where clinical judgments constitute the data? In this regard, W. A. Hunt [and those who have worked with him in this area of research, e.g., Hunt, Wittson and Hunt (1953) and Arnhoff (1954)] has maintained the position over the years that we should not consider the perception of data by the clinician as a separate and/or unique phenomenon, but, rather, as an instance of perceptual and judgmental processes, *sui generis*. Thus, we should expect that clinical judgment *should* be influenced by all the factors; judgments, in general, have been found to be influenced by, for example, personality of the rater, the influence of set, experimental conditions, and even the matrix of data in which the stimuli to be judged is embedded. And that, indeed, is exactly what we do find. Specifically, it has been found that significant differences in ratings result as a function of differences in professional training [e.g., Chance (1963), Elkin (1947), Grayson and Tolman (1950), Pumroy and Kogan (1955), Raskin et al. (1966), Stoller and Geertsma (1963), Strupp (1958a, b), Strupp and Williams (1960), Temerlin (1968), Wittenborn et al. (1961)], experience [e.g., Bendig and Sprague (1954), Gunderson (1965), Gunderson and Kapfer (1966), Nathan et al. (1969a), Hunt and Jones (1958), Jones (1957, 1959), Klehr (1949), Raskin et al. (1966, 1967)], or ability. [Clinicians have been found to vary in the general ability to make judgments, that is, vary in their perceptiveness.[23] Clinicians have also been found to be selectively sensitive to one or another facet of clinical phenomena, e.g., tests vs. directly observed behavior,[24] and some clinicians demonstrate a perceptual and/or conceptual bias in terms of "seeing" one form of psychopathology in their patients more so than other forms.][25] Clinical judgment has been found to have been influenced by the mental set of the clinician,[26] the very setting in which the clinician works,[27] and even by the nature of the scale in which the dimension is embedded.[28] Quite importantly, clinical judgment has been found to have been influenced by the degree to which the clinician likes or dislikes the patient.[29] In this latter regard, the judgments made by clinicians seem influenced by various socio-cultural stereotypes, as much as these influence ordinary social perception. For example, there seems little doubt any more about the fact that socio-cultural factors influence the form and content of the psychopathology as manifested by patients.[30] Thus, patients from the lower socio-economic level, even

[23] E.g., Grant et al. (1952), Gunderson (1965), Gunderson and Kapfer (1966), Holsopple and Phelan (1954), Hunt and Walker (1962), Hunt, Arnhoff and Cotton (1954), Katz, Cole and Lowery (1964, 1969), Kostlan, (1954), Nathan et al. (1969a), Pasamanick et al. (1959), Pepinsky (1948), Pumroy and Kogan (1955), Raines and Rohrer (1955, 1960), Ward et al. (1962), Watson and Logue (1968).

[24] E.g., Grant et al. (1952), Gunderson and Kapfer (1966), Holsopple and Phelan (1954), Hunt and Walker (1962), Katz, Cole and Lowery (1969).

[25] E.g., Ellis and Sells (1964), Goldfarb (1959), Gunderson and Kapfer (1966), Katz, Cole and Lowery (1969), Pasamanick et al. (1959), Pumroy and Kogan (1955), Raines and Rohrer (1955), with Raines and Rohrer suggesting that what clinicians tend not to see in their patients has to do with dimensions in themselves—perhaps the reverse is true also.

[26] E.g., Campbell et al. (1957), Chapman and Chapman (1967), Hunt and Arnhoff (1956), Hunt, Jones and Hunt (1957), Temerlin (1968).

[27] Whether that setting be a hospital or clinic [e.g., Babigian et al. (1965), Boisen (1938), Brill (1965a), Gunderson (1965), Hoch (1957), Nathan et al. (1969a), Siegel et al. (1963), Szasz (1957), Wilson and Meyer (1962)], or one country versus another [e.g., Gurland et al. (1970), Katz, Cole and Lowery (1969), Kendell et al. (1971), Simon et al. (1971)] where the sets may be different, as between different geographic areas of the same country [e.g., Spitzer et al. (1965)], or private practice [e.g., Goshen (1961), Hunt, Wittson and Hunt (1953), Szasz (1957, 1959)].

[28] E.g., Campbell et al. (1957), Rosenzweig et al. (1961).

[29] Robertson and Malchick (1968).

[30] E.g., Benedict (1934), Horney (1936), Montagu (1961), Opler (1955, 1959, 1963, 1967), Opler and Singer (1956a, b).

when diagnosed as neurotic, have been found to express their psychological problems somatically,[31] and tend to focus on situational factors rather than intrapsychic phenomena, i.e., their own motivational and attitudinal factors. A religious[32] and sexual[33] identity also seems to influence the form and content of the manifest psychopathology.[34] Clinicians respond to these stereotypes in particular ways, generally unfavorable. Thus, clinicians tend to diagnose the person from the lower socio-economic level as schizophrenic, while persons from the middle and upper levels tend to be diagnosed as neurotic.[35] Blacks,[36] Irish[37] and people from Hispanic ancestry[38] are very often viewed by their (very often white, Anglo-Saxon or Jewish) psychiatrists as more seriously disturbed than white, Anglo-Saxon patients. Patients from the lower socio-economic level *do* seem to expect their therapists to be more directive and to approach their problems from a "medical" rather than psychological point of view.[39] Thus, generally not finding this orientation in clinicians trained in exploratory psychotherapy and who are, to one degree or another, nondirective in their approach with patients

---

[31] Crandall and Dohrenwend (1967), Freedman and Hollingshead (1957), Moore *et al.* (1963), Rickels *et al.* (1966), Schwab *et al.* (1967), Yamamoto and Goin (1966).

[32] E.g., Murphy *et al.* (1967).

[33] E.g., Wittenborn and Smith (1964).

[34] Cultural factors seem to be so consistent an influence on the form and content of psychopathology that several investigators have explored the changes that can be observed with changes in cultures over time, e.g., Klaf and Hamilton (1961), Opler (1955) and Stainbrook (1954).

[35] E.g., Dunham (1964), Hollingshead and Redlich (1953, 1954, 1958), Hyde and Kingsley (1944), Kahn *et al.* (1966), Klerman and Paykel (1970), McDermott *et al.* (1965, 1967), Mendel and Rapport (1969), Michael (1967), Phillips *et al.* (1966), Raskin and Golob (1966), Redlich *et al.* (1953), Sabot *et al.* (1969), Schwartz and Errera (1963), Stenback and Achte (1966), Tietze *et al.* (1941), Williams *et al.* (1967).

[36] E.g., Brody (1961), DeHoyos and DeHoyos (1965), Fabrega *et al.* (1968), Gross *et al.* (1969), Karno (1966).

[37] E.g., Fantl and Schiro (1959), Opler and Singer (1956a, b), Roberts and Myers (1954).

[38] E.g., Dohrenwend (1966), Fabrega *et al.* (1968), Karno (1966), Meadow and Stoker (1965), Pokorny and Overall (1970).

[39] E.g., Overall and Aronson (1963), Rosenthal and Frank (1958), Williams *et al.* (1967).

the patients from the lower socio-economic level *do* tend to drop out of therapy earlier and more frequently than patients from the middle class.[40] Even though patients from the lower socio-economic level seem to profit as much from psychotherapy as their middle-class counterparts, if they remain long enough,[41] they are, *a priori*, viewed as being poor risks.[42] The statistics indicate that patients from the lower socio-economic group, at least up until recently, tend to be recommended not for psychotherapy, but, rather, chemotherapy and/or hospitalization. This bias extends even to the evaluation of test data [e.g., Auld (1952), Levy and Kahn (1970)]; the responses of patients from the lower socio-economic level are judged to be more reflective of psychopathology than those of patients from the middle class. It is, thus, apparent that some very real judgments and decisions in clinical work may not be a function of psychiatric diagnosis at all. Rather, it would seem that what would appear as an objective clinical decision may be a function of whether (perhaps unconsciously) the clinician likes or dislikes the patient, or whether the clinician can or cannot empathize with the patient. This preference (i.e., likeability[43]) seems to be a function of the socio-economic and socio-cultural background of the patient, which, itself, would seem to be a function of similarity of socio-economic and cultural backgrounds and/or personality type between clinician and patient, hence, identification. It has been found that the further away from the patient's socio-economic and socio-cultural background the clinician is (that is, the less he can identify with the patient), the less the clinician can seem to perceive the patient with objectivity and/or

[40] E.g., Auld and Meyers (1954), Brown and Kosterlitz (1964), Cole *et al.* (1962), Frank *et al.* (1957), Garfield and Affleck (1959, 1961), Imber *et al.* (1955), Lief *et al.* (1961), Lorr, Katz and Rubinstein (1958), Rosenthal and Frank (1958), Rubinstein and Lorr (1956), Storrow (1962), Sullivan *et al.* (1958), Turner (1968), Winder and Hersko (1955), Yamamoto and Goin (1966).

[41] E.g., Frank *et al.* (1957).

[42] E.g., Aronson and Overall (1966), Brill and Storrow (1960), Cole *et al.* (1962), Harrison *et al.* (1965), Lief *et al.* (1961), Michael (1967), Myers and Schaffer (1954), Rosenthal and Frank (1958), Schaffer and Myers (1954), Sullivan *et al.* (1958), Turner (1968).

[43] E.g., O'Malley (1917), Parloff (1956), Robertson and Malchick (1968), Robinson *et al.* (1954), Strupp (1958b), Thurrell and Levitt (1967), Wallach (1962), Wallach and Strupp (1960), Yamamoto *et al.* (1967).

without bias.[44] It should not be surprising, therefore, in the face of all these factors that do influence the conceptions and perceptions of the clinicians, inter-judge agreement tends to be low.[45] In summary, then, we have, now, seen that not only do outcome or life history data fail to show a consistent relationship with psychiatric diagnoses, but that clinicians do not use this schema as the criterion for making certain vital judgments concerning the patient's life.

Others have taken a look at this same body of research but, despite the conceptual and methodological difficulties, still see virtue in a classification schema and urge us to continue our research efforts to refine the classification system until it becomes viable [e.g., Brill (1965a), Cole (1965), Gardner (1965), Jenkins (1953), Katz, Cole and Barton (1965), Kety (1965), Menninger (1959b), Shakow (1965, 1966)]. Conferences continue to be called to attempt to stimulate new ideas [e.g., Hoch and Zubin (1953), Mahrer (1970)]. We *could* dwell on all those aspects of the research which need refining in order to sharpen our methodology (for example, improving the sampling, refining the inventories or behavioral observational scales, using sophisticated methods of statistical analysis, using computers to maximize data input and

---

[44] E.g., Chess *et al.* (1953), Gross *et al.* (1969). With the clinicians playing so significant a part in the outcome of a (clinical or research) study, one might begin to empathize somewhat with those who have looked to by-pass the clinician through such techniques as actuarial methods of prediction (e.g., Meehl, 1954, 1956, 1959), factor analysis (e.g., Marzolf, 1945), or the computer [e.g., Smith (1966), Spitzer and Endicott (1968), Spitzer *et al.* (1967)].

[45] E.g., the research by Arnhoff (1954), Arthur and Gunderson (1966a, b), Ash (1949), Babigian *et al.* (1965), Beck *et al.* (1962), Campbell *et al.* (1957), Cartwright and French (1939), Chance (1963), Datel and Gengerelli (1955), Doering and Raymond (1934), Edelman (1969), Elkin (1947), Gauron and Dickinson (1966a, b), Gertz *et al.* (1959), Goldfarb (1959), Gorham and Overall (1961), Grant *et al.* (1952), Guertin (1956b), Gunderson (1965), Gunderson and Kapfer (1966), Harris *et al.* (1963), Holsopple and Phelan (1954), Hunt and Walker (1962), Hunt, Arnhoff and Cotton (1954), Hunt, Jones and Hunt (1957), Katz, Cole and Lowery (1969), Kendell *et al.* (1971), Klehr (1949), Kreitman (1961), Kreitman *et al.* (1961), Meehl (1946, 1959), Mehlman (1952), Miller (1964), Nathan *et al.* (1969a), Pasamanick *et al.* (1959), Pumroy and Kogan (1955), Raines and Rohrer (1955, 1960), Ramzy and Pickard (1949), Rubin and Shontz (1960), Sandifer *et al.* (1964), Stoller and Geertsma (1963), Stone (1969), Stone and Skurdal (1968), Strupp (1958), Strupp and Williams (1960), Swensen (1957, 1968), Temerlin (1968), Ullman and Gurel (1962), Watson and Logue (1968). Moreover, the more specific the diagnostic decision, the lower the inter-rater agreement [e.g., Schmidt and Fonda (1956)].

processing, etc.), thereby hoping to enhance the possibility that we might get more positive results in support of the system of classification in psychiatry as being useful—but we will not. On the basis of what we have just concluded about the system of classification used in psychiatry, with the overwhelming lack of connectedness between diagnostic statements and life events, we *must* ask ourselves why we *should* expend further energies on refining a system that seems so useless. Why not expend those energies to attempt to establish those dimensions that *do* facilitate an understanding of the behavior of patients? In like mood, MacKinnon (1949) noted that although we could probably develop more accurate modes of diagnosing, this would not enhance our understanding of psychopathology. On the basis of our review of the relevant research, I feel that we must join forces with those who have forcibly spoken out against *diagnosing* as a process, e.g., Albee (1970), Cameron (1944), Rogers (1971), Szasz (1957a, b, 1959, 1961a, b, 1966), Winnicott (1965), etc.

This study can serve two purposes, viz., first, it can serve to strengthen the argument against diagnosing as regards psychopathology. At the expense of being repetitious, we have found that psychiatric diagnosing serves no practical purpose and does not enhance our understanding of psychopathology. To name is not to know [as Szasz (1961a) has already observed]. Second: the results of this study should create the climate for a healthy and (seemingly, most necessary) review and assessment of the assumptions that underlie our work in this field. We can no longer afford the luxury of ignoring the fact that clinical judgments, affecting the lives and welfare of other human beings, are being made, but not by the criterion (i.e., psychiatric diagnosis) by which we think they are being made. Obviously, sometimes these decisions are good ones, even though we may begin to question on what basis the clinician makes his judgments, and they facilitate the patient's psychological rehabilitation. However, if we are to lay claim to being scientific, we cannot tolerate such flagrant disregard for the basic principles of any scientific endeavor. (It also seems unfair to the patients, since the judgments seem highly personal on the part of the clinician.) Thus, we must harken to the cries of the philosophy of science people (e.g., Carnap, 1934) who have consistently asked that scientists recognize, question, and evaluate the assumptions which determine their work and conceptualizing.

Part of the problem with an applied arm of science, be it medicine, clinical psychology, engineering, etc., is that it tends to be an empirical endeavor. Confronted with the exigencies of daily problems, the applied scientist may have to try to resolve a situation without the (at least, adequate) help of research and theory. Most frequently, what has worked before is the first line of intervention; if that does not work, we will try something else, and if *that* does not work, perhaps we will stop and ask ourselves the important question: why? If the procedure works, we do not feel the need to confront the question of why it works: that is considered "academic". Sometimes one just does not have time to pose theoretical questions and/or test assumptions with adequate research; for example, there are patients who are in pain (physically or psychologically) *now*, and they need help, *now*. The reality of clinical work imposes a non-scientific approach. And if we say to our more research-oriented brethren: we will work as best as we can with what we have, you research the issue, we frequently distrust the research: it deals with part processes, segments of the human, limited facets of the entire situation, i.e., the totality of life in which this person is embedded; in short, "artificial". And so, without recourse to the very data that might modify our procedures for the better, we bungle on.

Through this study, we have come to find out that one procedure we use in clinical work, viz., diagnosing, is a procedure that proves to be virtually useless for working, for understanding. And yet, we cling to it *as if* it were necessary for both. Tradition.

Let us look at some of the assumptions that do underlie this procedure indeed, assumptions about the nature of Man that are inherent in this process [as have been confronted courageously by, for example, Cameron (1948), Dreger (1968), Finch (1966), Lewin (1931), Montagu (1955), Northrop (1948), Pratt and Tooley (1970), Sharma (1970), Vieth (1957), von Bertalanffy (1951) and Zilboorg (1954)]. Classification presumes ordering; an order presumes a reason for the ordering; a reason presumes some understanding. Thus, as regards Science, classification is the earmark of an advancement over simple observation. The diagnostic system in psychiatry is a classification system, and should convey the additional information of understanding that ordering one's data implies; it does not. Psychiatry, as a medical specialty, derives another pull towards such classifying since in medicine, a diagnosis *does* presume some knowledge about the symptoms being observed, other than that it might be associated with other symptoms. Our data suggest that in psychiatry, we have been duping ourselves. The system of classification for psychiatric events, i.e., psychopathology, does not, it turns out, provide the same information as does the classification system in medicine. *That is because the data are different and require a different approach.*

It is time that we in the social sciences stopped trying to fit our data or use methods into the (what has become a procrustean) bed of the physical sciences. (How many times have we heard that!) From our data, it becomes clear that it has not been fruitful to do so. Whereas in the physical sciences, the nature of the data permit of linear relationships (as regards, for example, cause and effect), in the social sciences, this is not possible. The complexity that is Man defies simplistic conceptualization, and yet we still keep trying. "Types of persons are difficult to define," wrote Adolf Meyer. "Once for all we should give up the idea of classifying as we classify plants" (Meyer, 1903, p. 91). And Fenichel has written:

> "The application of the general principles of natural science to the special field of psychology (creates) . . . a pseudo exactness which believes it necessary to transfer the biological methods of experiment and scientific protocol to a field where these methods are not suitable" (Fenichel, 1945, p. 7).

We need to note the insight of Spearman (1929), Thurstone (1934), George Klein (1948) or Eysenck (1955b) who have understood that identification of the data of Man necessitates a model that takes into account the multiplicity of events which determine any one, given behavior, *simultaneously*. And, moreover, that the identification of a given behavior, then, necessitates a geometric psychological space, with points on that grid for which no name suffices. Classification is an attempt, as Brill (1965b) stated, to reduce the "bewildering multiplicity of the subject matter", to undo what William James alluded to as the great buzzing confusion that is life. However, classification might only *seem* as though it has organized the data of a science meaningfully (until that organization is put to the test), lulling us into a false sense of security. The insightful amongst us, e.g. Maslow (1948), May (1971), Pearce and Newton (1963), and Szasz (1961a), to name but a few, had come to that insight already. It is time the rest of us did.

We must remember that when Kraeplin set about to classify the data of psychopathology, he was expecting his system not only to be descriptive, but to include etiological and prognostic considerations as well. As it turned out, that was an unrealistic goal. Karl Menninger has written:

> "A psychiatric diagnosis . . . is always a complex set of statements—descriptive, analytic and evaluative. They have to describe a patient's method of interacting with his environment, past and present . . . and . . . is always both polydimensional and multidisciplinary" (Menninger, 1959, pp. 233–234).

This necessity may be, however, a liability. For many [e.g., Cattell (1970), Gough (1971), Mahrer (1970d), Nathan (1967), Phillips and Rabinovitch (1958), Weisman (1965), Zilboorg (Zilboorg and Henry, 1941), Zubin (1965)] have indicated that one of the problems with psychiatric diagnosis *is* that the same system confounds various levels and facets of personality (e.g., etiological, phenomenological, cognitive, affective, social, psychodynamic, descriptive, etc.). In the face of this complexity, the pragmatic amongst us might recommend that since one system does not seem to fit all "occasions", perhaps a different mode of classifying would be necessary for each. Thus, we would have one system to describe, one to permit us to predict, and one to postdict. We know from other sources [e.g., Bowman and Rose (1951), Brill (1965a), Caverny *et al.* (1955), Gruenberg (1965), Jackson (1970), Meyer (1917), Szasz (1959), Zilboorg (Zilboorg and Henry, 1941)] that applied situations, e.g., clinical, judicial, social, etc., require different systems of classification of psychopathology, focusing on completely different facets of behavior. A decision a judge, a social worker, an administrator of a ward or a hospital, or a psychotherapist makes obviously does not focus on the same dimensions of personality or behavior. And we already know from research that the behavior of disturbed children groups into different categories than that of disturbed adults [e.g., Cameron (1955), Caverny *et al.* (1955), Chess (1960), Dreger (1964a, b), Dreger *et al.* (1964), Gruenberg (1965), Jenkins and Hewitt (1944), Kanner (1943, 1949), Noshpitz and Spielman (1961), Ransom and Gunderson (1966), Weil (1953)]. But this would be like throwing good money after bad (so to say): we have established that the system of classification used in psychiatry holds up *with regard to symptoms, but* that the symptom data do not contribute to our understanding of the patient or of psychopathology, *sui generis*. Why keep whipping a horse to race (to utilize another [admittedly bad] analogy) that should have been retired long ago?

Going beyond the diagnostic principle means discarding the inappropriate assumptions that have been *assumed* to be correct since they *are* correct for other approaches. Going beyond the diagnostic principle as regards the data of psychopathology means abandoning the posture of physical science or of medicine. Going beyond the diagnostic principle means recognizing that the data of psychopathology belong to the realm of psychology, not medicine, and must be approached from a psychological point of view.[46] We already have gleaned some insight from this study into some of the psychological dimensions that *do* relate to how a person is, was, and, perhaps, to some extent, will be, but we have hardly scratched the surface of such an understanding. Stevens (1936) has called psychology the propaedeutic science, and Eysenck (1955b) has suggested that psychology be to psychiatry what physiology is to internal medicine. It seems like it is up to the psychologist to try and make some meaningful contribution to psychiatry, but Stainbrook (1953) has pointed out that attempts to translate psychiatric phenomena into psychological goes as far back as the seventeenth and eighteenth centuries, and it is clear that the nineteenth and twentieth centuries have seen many such efforts. To be successful, one must fight

[46] That has always been (the seemingly unheeded) point of view of Kraeplin (lest we forget that he set out to develop a psychological interpretation of psychiatric phenomena—to the point of taking a degree in psychology under Wundt in order to do so), Adolf Meyer (e.g., 1904, 1912, 1917, 1926), as well as that of many others [e.g., Adams (1964), Albee (1970), Ausubel (1961), Babcock (1930, 1931), Beck (1964), Blitzstein (1938), Boisen (1938), Bordin (1946), Distler *et al.* (1965), Eysenck (e.g., 1951, 1955a, b, 1957, 1961, 1964, 1970; Eysenck and Claridge, 1963; Eysenck and Eysenck, 1969; Eysenck, Eysenck and Claridge, 1960), Fairbairn (1940, 1941), Glover (1957), Granger (1961), Grinker *et al.* (1968), Hausmann (1933), Herron (1963), Holt (1968), Holzberg and Wittenborn (1953), Hunt (1935, 1936), Ingham *et al.* (1964), Ittelson *et al.* (1961), Johannsen (1964), Kanfer and Saslow (1965), Kant (1940b), Karush *et al.* (1964), Langford (1964), Leary and Coffey (1955), Levine and Cohen (1962), Levine and Wittenborn (1970), Lorr (1953, 1966, 1970), MacKinnon (1949), Mahrer (1970b, c), Meldman (1964), Molish and Beck (1958a, b), Monro (1954), Murphy (1923), Payne (1961), Peters (1947), Rosanoff (1920), Sacks and Lewin (1950), Schilder (1933), Stainbrook (1953), Stephenson (1932a, b, c), Studman (1935), Szasz (1956, 1957), Thorne (e.g., 1949, 1953, 1964, 1967, 1970a, b; Thorne and Nathan, 1969, 1970), Watson (1951), Wells (1913, 1914).

against tradition: to be successful one must stop doing what *seems* to be correct, trying to accept the fact that the data argue against our continuing to diagnose. That would seem to take a monumental change in our belief systems as clinicians (and the therapists amongst us will tell us how difficult it is to change such systems, particularly when they *feel* right, though from a more objective point of view, one can demonstrate their inappropriateness). What we need, as regards the data of psychopathology, is the courage of a Ray Cattell who could abandon the traditional givens, and from a completely psychological frame of reference begin to try to determine the basic (and meaningful) traits and from these begin to organize the complexity of behavior, *de novo*. It is time to stop trying to be physicians of the body, and to recognize that we are physicians of the soul (*psyche*), i.e., psychologists, and focus on the psychological aspects of behavior in the study of psychopathology.

We already have some support for such a position; we have already seen that such variables as the level of psychosocial development prior to the overt manifestation of an acute disturbance (the so-called "good" and "poor" premorbid personality types or the "process" and "reactive" psychopathological types, both of which seem to relate to the same dimension, both of which seem to transcend particular diagnosis, at least in the psychotic range of behavior), the length of that time the acuteness of the disturbance exists, and the severity of the disturbance in its acute stage, are good predictors of outcome, and may be the more meaningful dimensions in trying to understand the nature of an individual's psychopathology or of psychopathology, *sui generis*. The process-reactive or good and poor premorbid personality types certainly not only describe current behavior, but describe the nature of events in individuals' life histories, as well as permit of some statement as regards prognosis and treatment. *These* are the sorts of dimensions for which Kraeplin sought; these satisfy all the requirements of his system of classification. These seem to order the data meaningfully, but it is still too early to know. Moreover, there are other psychological variables that research has found to be useful and meaningful as regards psychopathological states, e.g., the nature of an individual's current interpersonal relatedness,[47] motivational variables (Mahrer,

[47] E.g., Fairbairn (1941), Leary (Leary and Coffey, 1955; Leary, 1970), Kanfer and Saslow (1965).

1970b, c), ego strength,[48] and the very familiar introversion–extraversion.[49] Some research [e.g., Eskey and Friedman (1958), Eskey et al. (1957), Ey (1959), Glidewell et al. (1957), Hiler (1966), Kant (1944), Lewis (1938)] has indicated that the general degree of psychopathology is a variable that is correlated with prognosis, and, hence, may be a meaningful and useful dimension [and we already have scales which purport to measure such a dimension, e.g., Barron (1953), Blumberg (1967), Burdock and Hardesty (1968), Ellsworth and Clayton (1959), Goodrich (1953), Sines and Silver (1963), Tamkin (1959), and Watkins and Stauffacher (1952), and Hoover (1955) has presented us with a paper-and-pencil test measuring contact with reality]. Agel (1971) has commented that alienation is the core of all psychiatric difficulties; that all psychopathology is just a function of degree of alienation, and we have a scale (Davids, 1955) that purports to measure alienation. There seems to be little doubt that there is such a phenomenon as schizophrenia. However, rather than trying to differentiate schizophrenia into various psychiatric subtypes (which, although making us feel like we are making meaningful differentiations, proves to have little relevance to anything but a constellation of symptoms), a more meaningful dimension would seem to be the *degree* of schizophrenicity, i.e., of schizophrenic disorganization, that each person manifests. This would seem to relate more to prognosis in general, and with regard to treatment. Beginning with the work of Feifel (1949), Hunt (and his students) have attempted to refine a measure of degree of schizophrenicity derived from an assessment of the patient's attempts to define words, that is, tapping in to the thought disorder at its most vulnerable point for the schizophrenic [e.g., Hunt and Arnhoff (1955), Hunt and Jones (1958), Hunt and Walker (1962), Hunt, Walker and

[48] E.g., Distler et al. (1965), Fairbairn (1940), Glover (1957), Grinker et al. (1968), Holzberg and Wittenborn (1953), Karush et al. (1964), Levine and Cohen (1962), but most specifically, Menninger (e.g., Menninger, 1954a, b, c; Menninger et al., 1958, 1963).

[49] A factor which has held up over the years, clinically as well as in terms of research, but one which seems to have little current popularity [e.g., Allport and Allport (1921), Cattell (1933, 1943a, 1945a, b, 1947, 1956), Eysenck (1951, 1957, 1961, 1970), Eysenck and Eysenck (1969), Eysenck, Eysenck and Claridge (1960), Foulds (1959), Gard and Bendig (1964), Himmelweit et al. (1946), Horn (1944), Jung (1932), Lorr, Caffey and Gessner (1968), Mosier (1937)].

Jones (1960), Jones (1959)]. In a similar vein, there are ratings scales for degree of neuroticism [e.g., Thurstone and Thurstone (1930), Winne (1951)], or degree of susceptibility to stress (Stone, 1969), or of insecurity (Maslow *et al.*, 1945), or of interpersonal trust (Rotter, 1967), or of degree of anxiety [e.g., Buss *et al.* (1955), Taylor (1953)]. Perhaps in exploring depression, *degree* of depressiveness will be found to be a more meaningful dimension than the way we tend to think of depressive states now [a dimension for which we already have scales, e.g., Bayard and Pascal (1954), Beck *et al.* (1961), Cutler and Kurland (1961), Dempsey (1964), Hamilton (1960), Lubin (1965, 1966), Plutchik *et al.* (1970), Seitz (1970), Wechsler *et al.* (1963)]. Beginning with the work of Saul Rozenzweig (Rosenzweig, 1934), there has been much clinical work suggesting that the direction of a person's hostility may be an important dimension as regards the nature of their psychopathology and prognosis of their disorder [e.g., Albee (1950, 1951), Feldman *et al.* (1954), Marks *et al.* (1960), Thorne (1953)], or perhaps the degree of hostility one has [for which there are scales which purport to measure this dimension, e.g., Buss, Durkee and Baer (1956) or Siegel (1956)]. Phillips and Zigler (1964), Phillips *et al.* (1968), Zigler and Phillips (1960, 1962) all found that prognosis is related to that (latter) dimension; externalizers had a poorer prognosis than those who internalized their hostility. Meldman (1964) wants to offer a system of categorization of psychiatric data based on various kinds and degrees of disorders of attention, and Fairbairn (1941) suggested that classification of psychiatric disorder should be on the basis of the nature of a person's object relations. We should (and could) come up with other dimensions of personality which could be heuristic in the study of psychopathology. It is clear that we (still) need some basic research, exploring what is, defining the basic dimensions of this complex called psychopathology, *before* we go about the task of putting all this into some meaningful organization, arithmetic or geometric.

CHAPTER 9

EPILOGUE

WE have come to the end of our journey. We have coursed through the research. We have tried to touch as many of the points along the way that we should have. A conscientious and comprehensive survey of all the relevant studies of all the relevant dimensions seems to leave little doubt as to the outcome of our exploration. The data seem clear; the evidence weighs heavily against the system of classification used in psychiatry. This system turns out to be a purely descriptive one. To be useful, the diagnostic statements would have to provide information about the individual, something other than describing his symptoms; the classification system does not do this.

What we truly need, in the study of psychopathology, is a revolution. We have to throw off the conceptual shackles of ways of approaching data borrowed from the physical sciences and medicine which serve us ill. We have to think psychologically, and explore the phenomena of psychopathology from the point of view of the interpersonal as well as the intrapsychic, not just as regards the manifest behavior. Whether we will get such a revolution remains to be seen. Without it, we [i.e., the field of psychopathology (of which psychiatry is a part)] are doomed to an outmoded and, worse, inappropriate mode of conceptualization that contributes little if anything to the understanding of people. Our system of classification in psychiatry has proven to be: full of sound and fury, signifying nothing. Ernst Cassirer has written:

"The notion that name and essence bear a necessary and internal relation to each other, that the name does not merely denote but actually *is* the essence of its object, that the potency of the real thing is contained in the name—that is one of the fundamental assumptions of the mythmaking consciousness" (Cassirer, 1946, p. 3).

80

". . . all schema which science evolves in order to classify, organize, and summarize the phenomena of the real world turn out to be nothing but arbitrary schema—air fabrics of the mind . . ." (Cassirer, 1946, p. 7).

We can now state how unequivocally correct Cassirer was: diagnostic naming has proven to be a myth.

We end this course through the research like so many other critical reviews of clinical phenomena:

(a) on a note of skepticism concerning the validity of one of our hypotheses (in this instance, that psychiatric diagnoses are meaningful and useful statements); and
(b) calling for the proverbial: more research.

We should be concerned that so much of the time when we put our clinically derived hypotheses to the test, the data of research so often fail to confirm them. Of course it might be that the hypotheses derived from clinical data cannot be validated by research. Every clinician entertains that notion in order to justify ignoring that research which does not lend support to our cherished assumptions. On the other hand, the research might be correct; many of our hypotheses, though having face validity, may, in fact, be erroneous. Indeed, it is frightening to think that we clinicians may hold to beliefs about behavior which are invalid, much as do our patients. That would appear to be the situation with regard to diagnosing of psychiatric phenomena. This study suggests that the system has only face validity, and yet I am sure clinicians will go right on using it, ignoring the research. One wonders how many of our so cherished assumptions fall into the category of believable, but not true.

REFERENCES

ABRAMS, G. M., TAINTER, Z. C., and LHAMON, W. T. (1966) Percept assimilation and paranoid severity. *Archives of General Psychiatry*, **14**, 491–496.

ADAMS, H. B. (1964) Mental illness of interpersonal behavior? *American Psychologist*, **19**, 191–196.

ADLER, L. M. (1953) The relationship of marital status to incidence of and recovery from mental illness. *Social Forces*, **32**, 185–194.

AGEL, L. (1971) *The Radical Therapist*. New York: Ballantine Books.

ALBEE, G. W. (1950) Patterns of aggression in psychopathology. *Journal of Consulting Psychology*, **14**, 465–468.

ALBEE, G. W. (1951) The prognostic importance of delusions in schizophrenia. *Journal of Abnormal and Social Psychology*, **46**, 208–212.

ALBEE, G. W. (1970) Notes toward a position paper opposing psychodiagnosis. In A. R. Mahrer (Ed.), *New Approaches to Personality Classification*, pp. 385–395. New York: Columbia University Press.

ALDRICH, C. K., and COFFIN, M. (1948) Clinical studies in the Navy. I. Prediction value of social histories and the Harrower-Erickson Test. *Journal of Nervous and Mental Disease*, **108**, 36–44.

ALDRICH, C., KNIGHT, F., and COFFIN, M. (1949) Clinical studies of psychoses in the Navy. II. Prognoses. *Journal of Nervous and Mental Disease*, **108**, 142–148.

ALEXANDER, F., and SELESNICK, S. (1966) *The History of Psychiatry*. New York: Harper & Row.

ALEXANDER, G. H. (1945) Therapeutic efficacy of electroconvulsive therapy. *Journal of Nervous and Mental Disease*, **102**, 221–230.

ALLPORT, F. H., and ALLPORT, G. W. (1921) Personality traits: Their classification and measurement. *Journal of Abnormal and Social Psychology*, **16**, 6–40.

AMERICAN PSYCHIATRIC ASSOCIATION (1952) *Diagnosis and Statistical Manual of Mental Disorders*. Washington, D.C.

AMERICAN PSYCHIATRIC ASSOCIATION (1968) *Diagnostic and Statistical Manual of Mental Disorders*. Washington, D.C.

ARIETI, S. (1962) The psychotherapeutic approach to depression. *American Journal of Psychotherapy*, **16**, 397–406.

ARNHOFF, F. N. (1954) Some factors influencing the unreliability of clinical judgment. *Journal of Clinical Psychology*, **10**, 272–275.

ARTHUR, R. J., and GUNDERSON, E. K. E. (1966a) Stability in psychiatric diagnoses from hospital admissions to discharge. *Journal of Clinical Psychology*, **22**, 140–144.

ARTHUR, R. J., and GUNDERSON, E. K. E. (1966b) The prediction of diagnosis and disposition in naval hospitals. *Journal of Clinical Psychology*, **22**, 259–264.

ASH, P. (1949) The reliability of psychiatric diagnoses. *Journal of Abnormal and Social Psychology*, **44**, 272–276.

83

ASTRUP, C., FOSSUM, A., and HOLMBOE, R. (1962) *Prognoses in Functional Psychoses.* Springfield, Illinois: C. C. Thomas.

AULD, F. (1952) Influence of social class on personality test responses. *Psychological Bulletin*, **49**, 318–332.

AULD, F., and MEYERS, J. K. (1954) Contribution to a theory for selecting psychotherapy patients. *Journal of Clinical Psychology*, **10**, 56–60.

AUMACK, L. (1962) A social adjustment behavior rating scale. *Journal of Clinical Psychology*, **18**, 436–441.

AUMACK, L. (1969) The Patient Activity Checklist: An instrument and an approach for measuring behavior. *Journal of Clinical Psychology*, **25**, 134–137.

AUSUBEL, D. P. (1961) Personality disorder is disease. *American Psychologist*, **16**, 69–74.

BABCOCK, H. (1930) An experiment in the measure of mental deterioration. *Archives of Psychology*, **18**, No. 117.

BABCOCK, H. (1931) Psychological testing in psychopathology. *Journal of Applied Psychology*, **15**, 584–589.

BABIGIAN, H. M., GARDNER, E. A., MILES, H. C., and ROMANO, J. (1965) Diagnostic consistency and change in a followup study of 1,215 patients. *American Journal of Psychiatry*, **121**, 895–901.

BANNISTER, D., SALMON, P., and LEIBERMAN, D. M. (1964) Diagnosis–treatment relationships in psychiatry: A statistical analysis. *British Journal of Psychiatry*, **110**, 726–732.

BARBATO, L. (1942) Three years' experience with metrazol convulsive therapy (Results and follow-up studies in 167 cases). *Diseases of the Nervous System*, **3**, 250–256.

BARRON, F. (1953) Some test correlates of response to psychotherapy. *Journal of Consulting Psychology*, **17**, 235–241.

BAYARD, J., and PASCAL, G. R. (1954) Studies of prognostic criteria in the case records of hospitalized mental patients: Affective expression. *Journal of Consulting Psychology*, **18**, 122–126.

BECK, A. T., WARD, C. H., MENDELSON, M., MOCK, J., and ERBAUGH, J. (1961) An inventory for measuring depression. *Archives of General Psychiatry*, **4**, 561–571.

BECK, A. T., WARD, C. H., MENDELSON, M., MOCK, J. E., and ERBAUGH, J. K. (1962) Reliability of psychiatric diagnoses: 2. A study of consistency of clinical judgments and ratings. *American Journal of Psychiatry*, **119**, 351–357.

BECK, S. J. (1938) Personality structure in schizophrenia: A Rorschach investigation in 81 patients and 64 controls. *Nervous and Mental Disease Monographs*, No. 63.

BECK, S. J. (1954) *The Six Schizophrenias.* New York: American Orthopsychiatric Association.

BECK, S. J. (1964) Symptom and trait in schizophrenia. *American Journal of Orthopsychiatry*, **34**, 517–526.

BECKENSTEIN, N. (1939) Results of metrazol therapy in schizophrenia. *Psychiatric Quarterly*, **13**, 106–113.

BEIGEL, A., and MURPHY, D. L. (1971) Unipolar and bipolar affective illness. *Archives of General Psychiatry*, **24**, 215–220.

BEIGEL, A., MURPHY, D. L., and BUNNEY, W. E. (1971) The Manic-State Rating Scale: Scale construction, reliability, and validity. *Archives of General Psychiatry*, **25**, 256–262.

BENDIG, A. W., and HAMLIN, R. M. (1955) The psychiatric validity of an inverted factor analysis of Rorschach scoring categories. *Journal of Consulting Psychology*, **19**, 183–188.

BENDIG, A. W., and SPRAGUE, J. (1954) Rater experience and the reliability of case history ratings of adjustment. *Journal of Consulting Psychology*, **18**, 207–211.

BENEDICT, R. (1934) Anthropology and the abnormal. *Journal of General Psychology*, **10**, 58–82.

BERKOWITZ, M., and LEVINE, J. (1953) Rorschach scoring categories as diagnostic "signs". *Journal of Consulting Psychology*, **17**, 110–112.

BIANCHI, J. A., and CHIARELLO, C. J. (1944) Shock therapy in the involutional and manic-depressive psychoses. *Psychiatric Quarterly*, **18**, 118–126.

BIERI, J., ATKINS, A. L., BRIAR, S., LEAMAN, R. L., MILLER, H., and TRIPODI, T. (1966) *Clinical and Social Judgment: The Discrimination of Behavioral Information.* New York: Wiley.

BLEULER, E. (1950) *Dementia Praecox or the Group of Schizophrenias.* New York: International Universities Press.

BLINDER, M. G. (1966) The pragmatic classification of depression. *American Journal of Psychiatry*, **123**, 259–279.

BLITZSTEN, N. L. (1938) Psychoanalytic contributions to the conception of disorder types. *American Journal of Psychiatry*, **94**, 1431–1439.

BLUMBERG, S. (1967) MMPI F scale as an indicator of severity of psychopathology. *Journal of Clinical Psychology*, **23**, 96–99.

BOISEN, A. T. (1933) Experiential aspects of dementia praecox. *American Journal of Psychiatry*, **33**, 543–578.

BOISEN, A. T. (1938) Types of dementia praecox—A study in psychiatric classification. *Psychiatry*, **1**, 233–236.

BOND, E. D. (1941) Continued follow-up results in insulin-shock therapy and in control cases. *American Journal of Psychiatry*, **97**, 1024–1028.

BOND, E. D., and BRACELAND, F. J. (1937) Prognosis in mental disease. *American Journal of Psychiatry*, **94**, 263–274.

BOND, E. D., and RIVERS, T. D. (1942) Further follow-up results in insulin-shock therapy. *American Journal of Psychiatry*, **99**, 201–202.

BOND, E. D., and RIVERS, T. D. (1944) Insulin shock therapy after seven years. *American Journal of Psychiatry*, **101**, 62–63.

BONNER, C. A., and KENT, G. H. (1936) Overlapping symptoms in catatonic excitement and manic excitement. *American Journal of Psychiatry*, **92**, 1311–1322.

BORDIN, E. S. (1946) Diagnosis in counseling and psychotherapy. *Educational and Psychological Measurement*, **6**, 169–184.

BOSTIAN, D. W., SMITH, P. A., LASKY, J. J., HOVER, G. L., and GING, R. J. (1959) Empirical observations on mental-status examination. *Archives of General Psychiatry*, **1**, 253–262.

BOWER, P. A., TESTIN, R., and ROBERTS, A. (1960) Rorschach diagnosis by a systematic combining of content, thought process, and determinant scales. *Genetic Psychological Monographs*, **62**, 105–183.

BOWMAN, K. M., and ROSE, M. (1951) A criticism of the terms "psychosis," "psychoneurosis," and "neurosis." *American Journal of Psychiatry*, **108**, 161–166.

BOWMAN, K. M., WORTIS, J., FINGERT, H., and KAGAN, J. (1939) Results to date with the pharmacological shock treatment of schizophrenia. *American Journal of Psychiatry*, **95**, 787–791.

BRADWAY, K., and HEISLER, V. (1953) The relation between diagnosis and certain types of extreme deviations and content on the Rorschach. *Journal of Projective Techniques*, **17**, 70–74.

BRECHER, S. (1946) The value of diagnostic signs for schizophrenia on the Wechsler–Bellevue intelligence test. *Psychiatric Quarterly Supplement*, **20**, 58–64.

BRILL, H. (1965a) The role of classification in hospital psychiatry. In M. M. Katz, J. O. Cole, and W. E. Barton (Eds.), *The Role and Methodology of Classification in Psychiatry and Psychopathology*, pp. 29–35. Washington, D.C.: U.S. Government Printing Office.

BRILL, H. (1965b) Psychiatric diagnosis, nomenclature, and classification. In B. B. Wolman (Ed.), *Handbook of Clinical Psychology*, pp. 639–650. New York: McGraw-Hill.

BRILL, N. Q., and STORROW, H. A. (1960) Social class and psychiatric treatment. *Archives of General Psychiatry*, **3**, 240–244.

BRILL, N. Q., CRUMPTON, E., EIDUSON, S., GRAYSON, H. M., and HOLLMAN, L. I. (1959) Predictive and concomitant variables related to improvement with actual and simulated ECT. *Archives of General Psychiatry*, **1**, 263–272.

BRODY, E. B. (1961) Social conflict and schizophrenic behavior in young adult Negro males. *Psychiatry*, **24**, 337–346.

BROWN, J. S., and KOSTERLITZ, N. (1964) Selection and treatment of psychiatric outpatients: Determined by their personal and social characteristics. *Archives of General Psychiatry*, **11**, 425–438.

BULLARD, D. M. (1960) Psychotherapy of paranoid patients. *Archives of General Psychiatry*, **2**, 137–141.

BURDOCK, E. I., and HARDESTY, A. S. (1968) Psychological test for psychopathology. *Journal of Abnormal Psychology*, **73**, 62–69.

BUSS, A. H., DURKEE, A., and BAER, M. B. (1956) The measurement of hostility in clinical situations. *Journal of Abnormal and Social Psychology*, **52**, 84–86.

BUSS, A. H., WIENER, M., DURKEE, A., and BAER, M. (1955) The measurement of anxiety in clinical situations. *Journal of Consulting Psychology*, **19**, 125–129.

CALHOUN, J. F. (1971) Comment on differentiating paranoid from nonparanoid schizophrenics. *Journal of Consulting and Clinical Psychology*, **36**, 104–105.

CAMERON, D. E. (1948) The current transition in the conception of science. *Science*, **107**, 553–558.

CAMERON, D. E. (1953) A theory of diagnosis. In P. H. Hoch and J. Zubin (Eds.), *Current Problems in Psychiatric Diagnosis*, pp. 385–395. New York: Grune & Stratton.

CAMERON, K. (1955) Diagnostic categories in child psychiatry. *British Journal of Medical Psychology*, **28**, 67–71.

CAMERON, N. (1944) The functional psychoses. In J. McV. Hunt (Ed.), *Personality and the Behavior Disorders*, pp. 861–921. New York: Ronald Press.

CAMPBELL, D. T., HUNT, W. A., and LEWIS, N. A. (1957) The effects of assimilation and control in judgments of clinical materials. *American Journal of Psychology*, **70**, 347–360.

CANCRO, R. (1969) Prospective prediction of hospital stay in schizophrenia. *Archives of General Psychiatry*, **20**, 541–546.

CANCRO, R., and SUGERMAN, A. A. (1968) Classification and outcome in process-reactive schizophrenia. *Comprehensive Psychiatry*, **9**, 227–232.

CARNEY, M. W. P., ROTH, M., and GARSIDE, R. T. (1965) The diagnosis of depressive symptoms and the prediction of E.C.T. response. *British Journal of Psychiatry*, **111**, 659–674.

CARTWRIGHT, D., and FRENCH, J. R. P. (1939) The reliability of life-history studies. *Character and Personality*, **8**, 110–119.

CASSIRER, E. (1946) *Language and Myth*. Harper & Brothers.

CATTELL, R. B. (1933) Temperament tests: I. Temperament. *British Journal of Psychology*, **23**, 308–329.

CATTELL, R. B. (1943a) The description of personality: Basic traits resolved into clusters. *Journal of Abnormal and Social Psychology*, **38**, 476–506.

CATTELL, R. B. (1943b) The description of personality. I. Foundations of trait measurement. *Psychological Review*, **50**, 559–594.

CATTELL, R. B. (1945a) The description of personality: Principles and findings in a factor analysis. *American Journal of Psychology*, **58**, 69–90.

CATTELL, R. B. (1945b) The principal trait clusters for describing personality: I. The nature of personality description through clusters. *Psychological Bulletin*, **42**, 129–161.

CATTELL, R. B. (1947) Confirmation and classification of primary personality factors. *Psychometrika*, **12**, 197–220.

CATTELL, R. B. (1955) The principal replicated factors discovered in objective personality tests. *Journal of Abnormal and Social Psychology*, **50**, 291–314.

CATTELL, R. B. (1956) Second-order personality factors in the questionnaire realm. *Journal of Consulting Psychology*, **20**, 411–418.

CATTELL, R. B. (1957) The conceptual and test distinction of neuroticism and anxiety. *Journal of Clinical Psychology*, **13**, 221–233.

CATTELL, R. B. (1970) The integration of functional and psychometric requirements in a quantitative and computerized diagnostic system. In A. Maher (Ed.), *New Approaches to Personality Classification*, pp. 9–52. New York: Columbia University Press.

CATTELL, R. B., and SAUNDERS, D. R. (1950) Interpretation and matching of personality factors from behavior rating, questionnaire, and objective test data. *Journal of Social Psychology*, **31**, 243–260.

CATTELL, R. B., and SCHEIER, I. H. (1961) *The Nature and Measurement of Neuroticism and Anxiety*. New York: Ronald Press.

CATTELL, R. B., DUBIN, S. S., and SAUNDERS, D. R. (1954a) Verification of hypothesized factors in 115 objective personality test designs. *Psychometrika*, **19**, 209–230.

CATTELL, R. B., DUBIN, S. S., and SAUNDERS, D. R. (1954b) Personality structure in psychotics by factorization of objective clinical tests. *Journal of Mental Science*, **100**, 153–176.

CAVERNY, E. L., WITTSON, C., HUNT, W. A., and HERRMAN, R. F. (1955) Psychiatric diagnosis, its nature and function. *Journal of Nervous and Mental Disease*, **121**, 367–380.

CHANCE, E. (1963) Implications in interdisciplinary differences in case description. *American Journal of Orthopsychiatry*, **33**, 672–677.

CHAPMAN, L. J., and CHAPMAN, J. P. (1967) Genesis of popular but erroneous psychodiagnostic observations. *Journal of Abnormal Psychology*, **72**, 193–204.

CHAPMAN, L. J., DAY, D., and BURSTEIN, A. (1961) The process-reactive distinction and prognosis in schizophrenia. *Journal of Nervous and Mental Disease*, **133**, 383–391.

CHASE, L. S., and SILVERMAN, S. (1943) Prognosis in schizophrenia: An analysis of prognostic criteria in 150 schizophrenics treated with metrazol or insulin. *Journal of Nervous and Mental Disease*, **98**, 464–473.

CHENEY, C. O., and CLOW, H. E. (1941) Prognostic factors in insulin shock therapy. *American Journal of Psychiatry*, **97**, 1029–1039.

CHENEY, C. O., and DREWRY, P. H. (1930) Results of non-specific treatment in dementia praecox. *American Journal of Psychiatry*, **95**, 203–217.

CHESS, S. (1960) Diagnosis and treatment of the hyperactive child. *New York Journal of Medicine*, **60**, 2379–2385.

CHESS, S. K., CLARK, K. B., and THOMAS, A. (1953) The importance of cultural evaluation in psychiatric diagnosis and treatment. *Psychiatric Quarterly*, **27**, 102–114.

CHODOFF, P., and LYONS, H. (1958) Hysteria, the hysterical personality and "hysterical" conversion. *American Journal of Psychiatry*, **114**, 737–740.

CLOW, H. E. (1953) The use of a prognostic index of capacity for social adjustment in psychiatric disorders. In P. H. Hoch and J. Zubin (Eds.), *Current Problems in Psychiatric Diagnosis*, pp. 89–106. New York: Grune & Stratton.

CLUM, G. A., and HOIBERG, A. L. (1971) Prognostic indexes in a military psychiatric population. *Journal of Consulting and Clinical Psychology*, **36**, 436–440.

COHEN, H. (1943) The nature, methods and purpose of diagnosis. *Lancet*, **244**, 23–25.

COHEN, J. (1952) Factors underlying Wechsler–Bellevue performance of three neuropsychiatric groups. *Journal of Abnormal and Social Psychology*, **47**, 359–365.

COHEN, J., GUREL, L., and STUMPF, J. C. (1966) Dimensions of psychiatric symptom ratings determined at thirteen timepoints from hospital admission. *Journal of Consulting Psychology*, **30**, 39–44.

COHEN, L. H., MALMO, R. B., and THALE, T. (1944) Measurement of chronic psychotic over-activity by the Norwich Scale. *Journal of General Psychology*, **30**, 65–74.

COLE, J. O. (1965) Classification in research on the prediction of response to specific treatments in psychiatry. In M. M. Katz, J. O. Cole, and W. E. Barton (Eds.), *The Role and Methodology of Classification in Psychiatry and Psychopathology*, pp. 143–147. Washington, D.C.: U.S. Government Printing Office.

COLE, M. E., SWENSEN, C. H., and PASCAL, G. R. (1954) Prognostic significance of precipitating stress in mental illness. *Journal of Consulting Psychology*, **18**, 171–175.

COLE, N. J., BRANCH, C. H., and ARLISON, R. B. (1962) Some relationship between social class and practice of dynamic therapy. *American Journal of Psychiatry*, **118**, 1004–1012.

COMREY, A. L. (1957a) A factor analysis of items on the MMPI Hypochondriasis Scale. *Education and Psychological Measurement*, **17**, 568–577.

COMREY, A. L. (1957b) A factor analysis of items on the MMPI Depression Scale. *Educational and Psychological Measurement*, **17**, 578–585.

COMREY, A. L. (1957c) A factor analysis of items on the MMPI Hysteria Scale. *Educational and Psychological Measurement*, **17**, 586–592.

COMREY, A. L. (1958a) A factor analysis of items on the MMPI Paranoia Scale. *Educational and Psychological Measurement*, **18**, 99–107.

COMREY, A. L. (1958b) A factor analysis of items on the MMPI Psychasthenia Scale. *Educational and Psychological Measurement*, **18**, 293–300.

COMREY, A. L. (1958c) A factor analysis of items on the MMPI Hypomania Scale. *Educational and Psychological Measurement*, **18**, 313–323.

COMREY, A. L. (1962) Factored homogenous item dimensions: A strategy for personality research. In S. Messick and J. Ross (Eds.), *Measurement in Personality and Cognition*, pp. 11–26. New York: Wiley.

COMREY, A. L., and MARGGRAFF, W. M. (1958) A factor analysis of items on the MMPI Schizophrenia Scale. *Educational and Psychological Measurement*, **18**, 301–311.

COTTLE, W. C. (1950) A factorial study of the Multiphasic, Strong, Kuder, and Bell inventories using a population of adult males. *Psychometrika*, **15**, 25–47.

COUNTS, R. N., and DEVLIN, J. B. (1954) Sexual experience as a prognostic factor in psychosis. *Journal of Nervous and Mental Disease*, **120**, 364–368.

CRANDALL, D. L., and DOHRENWEND, B. P. (1967) Some relations among psychiatric symptoms, organic illness, and social class. *American Journal of Psychiatry*, **123**, 1527–1538.

CROPLEY, A. J., and WECKOWICZ, T. E. (1966) The dimensionality of clinical depression. *Australian Journal of Psychology*, **18**, 18–25.

CUTLER, R. P., and KURLAND, H. D. (1961) Clinical quantification of depressive reactions. *Archives of General Psychiatry*, **5**, 280–285.

DAHLSTROM, W. G., and PRANGE, A. J. (1960) Characteristics of depressive and paranoid schizophrenic reactions on the MMPI. *Journal of Nervous and Mental Disease*, **126**, 513–522.

DANA, R. H. (1957) Manifest anxiety, intelligence, and psychopathology. *Journal of Consulting Psychology*, **21**, 38–40.

DANZIGER, L., and KINDWALL, J. A. (1946) Prediction of immediate outcome of shock therapy in dementia praecox. *Disease of the Nervous System*, **7**, 299–303.

DATEL, W. E., and GENGERELLI, J. A. (1955) Reliability of Rorschach interpretation. *Journal of Projective Techniques*, **19**, 372–381.

DAVIDS, A. (1955) Alienation, social apperception, and ego structure. *Journal of Consulting Psychology*, **19**, 21–27.

DAVIS, W. E., DIZZONNE, M. F., and DEWOLFE, A. S. (1971) Relationships among WAIS subtest scores, patient's premorbid history, and institutionalization. *Journal of Consulting and Clinical Psychology*, **36**, 400–403.

DAWSON, J. G., and WEINGOLD, H. P. (1966) Prognostic significance of delusions in schizophrenics. *Journal of Clinical Psychology*, **22**, 275–277.

DAWSON, J. G., HINE, F. R., WRUSTER, C. R., and BRYANT, J. H. (1958) Clinical implications of factors derived from the Southeast Louisiana Hospital Rating Scale. *Journal of Psychology*, **46**, 175–178.

DEGAN, J. W. (1952) Dimensions of functional psychosis. *Psychometric Monographs*, No. 6.

DEHOYOS, A., and DEHOYOS, G. (1965) Symptomatology differentials between Negro and White schizophrenics. *International Journal of Social Psychiatry*, **11**, 245–255.

DEMPSEY, P. (1964) A unidimensional depression scale for the MMPI. *Journal of Consulting Psychology*, **28**, 364–370.

DEROGATIS, L. R., LIPMAN, R. S., COVI, L., RICKELS, K., and UHLENHUTH, E. H. (1970) Dimensions of outpatient neurotic pathology: Comparison of a clinical versus an empirical assessment. *Journal of Consulting and Clinical Psychology*, **34**, 164–171.

DIETHELM, O. (1953) The fallacy of the concept: psychosis. In P. H. Hoch and J. Zubin (Eds.), *Current Problems in Psychiatric Diagnosis*, pp. 24–32. New York: Grune & Stratton.

DIMMICK, G. B. (1935) An application of the Rorschach ink blot test to three clinical types of dementia praecox. *Journal of Psychology*, **1**, 61–74.

DISTLER, L. S., MAY, P. R. A., and TUMAN, A. H. (1965) Anxiety and ego strength as predictors of response to treatment in schizophrenic patients. *Journal of Consulting Psychology*, **29**, 565–570.

DOERING, C. R., and RAYMOND, A. F. (1934) Reliability of observation in psychiatric and related characteristics. *American Journal of Orthopsychiatry*, **4**, 249–257.

DOHRENWEND, B. P. (1966) Social status and disorder: An issue of substance and an issue of method. *American Sociological Review*, **31**, 14–34.

DOWNING, R. W., and RICKELS, K. (1965) Q-sort patterns of self-evaluation in three neurotic clinic populations. *Journal of Clinical Psychology*, **21**, 89–96.

DREGER, R. M. (1964a) A progress report on a factor analytic approach to classification in child psychiatry. In R. L. Jenkins and J. O. Cole (Eds.), *Diagnostic Classification in Child Psychiatry*, pp. 22–58. Washington, D.C.: American Psychiatric Association.

DREGER, R. M. (1964b) A progress report on a factor analytic approach to classification in child psychiatry. *Psychiatric Research Reports*, **18**, 22–58.

DREGER, R. M. (1968) Aristotle, Linnaeus, and Lewin, or the place of classification in the evaluative-therapeutic process. *Journal of General Psychology*, **78**, 41–59.

DREGER, R. M., REID, M. P., LEWIS, P. M., OVERLADE, D. C., RICH, T. A., TAFFEL, C., MILLER, K. S., and FLEMING, E. (1964) Behavioral classification project. *Journal of Consulting Psychology*, **28**, 1–13.

DUNHAM, H. W. (1964) Social class and schizophrenia. *American Journal of Orthopsychiatry*, **34**, 634–642.

DUNHAM, H. W., and MELTZER, B. N. (1946) Predicting length of hospitalization of mental patients. *American Journal of Sociology*, **52**, 123–131.

EASSER, B. R., and LESSER, S. R. (1965) Hysterical personality: A re-evaluation. *Psychoanalytic Quarterly*, **34**, 390–405.

EDELMAN, R. I. (1969) Intra-therapist diagnostic reliability. *Journal of Clinical Psychology*, **25**, 394–396.

ELKIN, F. (1947) Specialists interpret the case of Harold Holzer. *Journal of Abnormal and Social Psychology*, **42**, 99–111.

ELLIS, N. C., and SELLS, S. B. (1964) An analysis of psychiatric diagnosis in a military mental hygiene clinic. *Journal of Clinical Psychology*, **20**, 354–356.

ELLSWORTH, R. B., and CLAYTON, W. H. (1959) Measurement of improvement in "mental illness." *Journal of Consulting Psychology*, **23**, 15–20.

EPSTEIN, J. (1943) Electric shock therapy in the psychoses. *Journal of Nervous and Mental Disease*, **98**, 115–129.

ESKEY, A., and FRIEDMAN, I. (1958) The prognostic significance of certain behavioral variables. *Journal of Consulting Psychology*, **22**, 91–94.

ESKEY, A., FRIEDMAN, G. M., and FRIEDMAN, I. (1957) Distortion as a prognostic criterion. *Journal of Consulting Psychology*, **21**, 149–151.

EY, H. (1959) Unity and diversity of schizophrenia: Clinical and logical analysis of the concept of schizophrenia. *American Journal of Psychiatry*, **115**, 706–714.

EYSENCK, H. J. (1944) Types of personality—a factorial study of 700 neurotics. *Journal of Mental Science*, **90**, 851–861.

EYSENCK, H. J. (1951) The organization of personality. *Journal of Personality*, **20**, 101–117.

EYSENCK, H. J. (1952a) Schizothymia-cyclothymia as a dimension of personality: II. Experimental. *Journal of Personality*, **20**, 345–384.

EYSENCK, H. J. (1952b) *The Scientific Study of Personality*. London: Routledge & Kegan Paul.

EYSENCK, H. J. (1955a) Psychiatric diagnosis as a psychological and statistical problem. *Psychological Reports*, **1**, 3–17.

EYSENCK, H. J. (1955b) *Psychology and the Foundations of Psychiatry*. London: H. K. Lewis.

EYSENCK, H. J. (1955c) A dynamic theory of anxiety and hysteria. *Journal of Mental Science*, **101**, 28–51.

EYSENCK, H. J. (1957) *The Dynamics of Anxiety and Hysteria*. London: Routledge & Kegan Paul.

EYSENCK, H. J. (1961) Classification and the problem of diagnosis. In *Handbook of Abnormal Psychology*, pp. 1–31. New York: Basic Books.

EYSENCK, H. J. (1964) Principles and methods of personality description, classification and diagnosis. *British Journal of Psychology*, **55**, 284–294.

EYSENCK, H. J. (1970) A dimensional system of psychodiagnosis. In A. R. Mahrer (Ed.), *New Approaches to Personality Classification*, pp. 169–207. New York: Columbia University Press.

EYSENCK, H. J., and CLARIDGE, G. (1962) The position of hysterics and dysthymics in a two-dimensional framework of personality description. *Journal of Abnormal and Social Psychology*, **64**, 46–55.

EYSENCK, H. J., and EYSENCK, S. B. G. (1969) *Personality Structure and Measurement*. London: Routledge & Kegan Paul.

EYSENCK, S. B. G. (1956) Neurosis and psychosis: An experimental analysis. *Journal of Mental Science*, **102**, 517–529.

EYSENCK, S. B. G., and EYSENCK, H. J. (1968) The measurement of psychoticism: A study of factor stability and reliability. *British Journal of Social and Clinical Psychology*, **7**, 286–294.

EYSENCK, S. B. G., EYSENCK, H. J., and CLARIDGE, G. (1960) Dimensions of personality, psychiatric syndromes, and mathematical models. *Journal of Mental Science*, **106**, 581–589.

FABREGA, H., SWARTZ, J. D., and WALLACE, C. A. (1968) Ethnic differences in psychopathology. *Archives of General Psychiatry*, **19**, 218–226.

FAIRBAIRN, W. R. D. (1941) A revised psychopathology of the psychoses and psychoneuroses. *International Journal of Psychoanalysis*, **22**, 250–279.

FAIRBAIRN, W. R. D. (1952) Schizoid factors in the personality (1940). In *Psychoanalytic Studies of the Personality*, pp. 3–27. London: Tavistock Publications, Ltd.

FAIRWEATHER, G. W., MORAN, L. J., and MORTON, R. B. (1956) Efficiency of attitudes, fantasies, and life history data in predicting observed behavior. *Journal of Consulting Psychology*, **20**, 58.

FAIRWEATHER, G. W., SIMON, R., GEBHARD, M. E., WEINGARTEN, W., HOLLAND, J. L., SANDERS, R., STONE, C. D., and REAHL, J. E. (1960) A multi-criteria comparison of the relative efficiency of four psychotherapeutic programs for three different patient groups. *Psychological Monographs*, **74**, Whole No. 492.

FANTL, B., and SCHIRO, J. (1959) Cultural variables in the behavior patterns and symptom formation of 15 Irish and 15 Italian female schizophrenics. *International Journal of Social Psychiatry*, **4**, 245–253.

FARINA, A., and WEBB, W. W. (1956) Premorbid adjustment and subsequent discharge. *Journal of Nervous and Mental Disease*, **124**, 612–613.

FARINA, A., GARMEZY, N., and BARRY, H. (1963) Relationship of marital status to incidence and prognosis of schizophrenia. *Journal of Abnormal and Social Psychology*, **67**, 624–630.

FARINA, A., GARMEZY, N., ZALUSKY, M., and BECKER, J. (1962) Premorbid behavior and prognosis in female schizophrenic patients. *Journal of Consulting Psychology*, **26**, 56–60.

FEIFEL, H. (1949) Qualitative differences in the vocabulary responses of normals and abnormals. *Genetic Psychological Monographs*, **39**, 151–204.

FELDMAN, D. A., PASCAL, G. R., and SWENSEN, C. H. (1954) Direction of aggression as a prognosis variable in mental illness. *Journal of Consulting Psychology*, **18**, 167–170.

FENICHEL, O. (1945) *The Psychoanalytic Theory of Neurosis*. New York: Norton.

FERGUSON, J. T., McREYNOLDS, P., and BALLACHEY, E. L. (1953) *Hospital Adjustment Scale*. Palo Alto, California: Leland Stanford Junior University.

FINCH, J. R. (1966) Scientific models and their application in psychiatric models. *Archives of General Psychiatry*, **15**, 1–6.

FINE, R. (1968) Interpretation: The patient's response. In E. F. Hammer (Ed.), *Use of Interpretation in Treatment: Technique and Art*, pp. 110–120. New York: Grune & Stratton.

FINE, R. (1970) Therapeutic accessibility as a basis for diagnosis. In A. R. Mahrer (Ed.), *New Approaches to Personality Classification*, pp. 121–136. New York: Columbia University Press.

FISHER, S. (1951) Rorschach patterns in conversion hysteria. *Journal of Projective Techniques*, **15**, 98–108.

FISKE, D. W. (1956) A plea for more research and less diagnosis. *Psychological Reports*, **2**, 409–412.

FOULDS, G. A. (1959) The relative stability of personality measures compared with diagnostic measures. *Journal of Mental Science*, **105**, 783–787.

FOULDS, G. A. (1961) Personality traits and neurotic symptoms and signs. *British Journal of Medical Psychology*, **37**, 1–8.

FOULDS, G. A. (1962) A quantification of diagnostic differentia. *Journal of Mental Science*, **108**, 389–405.

FOULDS, G. A. (1964) Personal continuity and psychopathological disruption. *British Journal of Psychology*, **55**, 269–276.

FOULDS, G. A. (1965) *Personality and Personal Illness*. London: Tavistock Publications.

FOULDS, G. A., and CAINE, T. M. (1958) Psychoneurotic symptom clusters, trait clusters and psychological tests. *Journal of Mental Science*, **104**, 722–731.

FOULDS, G. A., and CAINE, T. M. (1959) Symptom clusters and personality types among psychoneurotic men compared with women. *Journal of Mental Science*, **105**, 469–475.

FOULDS, G. A., and OWEN, A. (1963) Are paranoids schizophrenics? *British Journal of Psychiatry*, **109**, 674–679.

FRANK, G. H. (1956) The Wechsler–Bellevue and psychiatric diagnosis: A factor analytic approach. *Journal of Consulting Psychology*, **20**, 67–69.

FRANK, G. H. (1965) The role of the family in the development of psychopathology. *Psychological Bulletin*, **64**, 191–205.

FRANK, G. H. (1970) On the nature of borderline psychopathology: A review. *Journal of General Psychology*, **83**, 61–77.

FRANK, G. H., CORRIE, C. C., and FOGEL, J. (1955) An empirical critique of research with the Wechsler–Bellevue in differential psychodiagnosis. *Journal of Clinical Psychology*, **11**, 291–293.

FRANK, J. D., GLIEDMAN, L. H., IMBER, S. D., NASH, E. H., and STONE, A. R. (1957) Why patients leave psychotherapy. *Archives of Neurology and Psychiatry*, **77**, 283–299.

FREEDMAN, L. Z., and HOLLINGSHEAD, A. B. (1957) Neurosis and social class: I. Social interaction. *American Journal of Psychiatry*, **113**, 769–775.

FREUD, S. (1958a) Observations on "wild" psychoanalysis (1910). *Standard Edition of the Complete Psychological Works of Sigmund Freud*. Vol. 11, pp. 221–227. London: Hogarth Press.

FREUD, S. (1958b) Further recommendations in the technique of psychoanalysis: On beginning the treatment. The question of the first communication. The dynamics of the cure (1913). *Standard Edition of the Complete Psychological Works of Sigmund Freud*. Vol. 12, pp. 123–144. London: Hogarth Press.

FREUDENBERG, R. K., and ROBERTSON, J. P. S. (1956) Symptoms in relation to psychiatric diagnosis and treatment. *Archives of Neurology and Psychiatry*, **76** 14–22.

FRIEDMAN, A. S., COWITZ, B., COHEN, H. W., and GRANICK, S. (1963) Syndromes and themes of psychotic depression. *Archives of General Psychiatry*, **9**, 504–509.

FRIEDMAN, H. (1952) A comparison of a group of hebephrenic and catatonic schizophrenics with two groups of normal adults by means of certain variables of the Rorschach test. *Journal of Projective Techniques*, **16**, 352–360.

FULLER, R. (1930) Expectation of hospital life and outcome for mental patients on first admission. *Psychiatric Quarterly*, **4**, 295–323.

FULLER, R., and JOHNSTON, M. (1931a) The duration of hospital life for mental patients. *Psychiatric Quarterly*, **5**, 341–352.

FULLER, R., and JOHNSTON, M. (1931b) The duration of hospital life for mental patients. *Psychiatric Quarterly*, **5**, 552–582.

FULTON, J. R., and LOREI, T. W. (1967) Predicting length of psychiatric hospitalization from history records. *Journal of Clinical Psychology*, **23**, 218–221.

GARD, J. G., and BENDIG, A. W. (1964) A factor analytic study of Eysenck's and Schutz's personality dimensions among psychiatric groups. *Journal of Consulting Psychology*, **28**, 252–258.

GARDNER, E. A. (1965) The role of the classification system in outpatient psychiatry. In M. M. Katz, J. O. Cole, and W. E. Barton (Eds.), *The Role and Methodology of Classification in Psychiatry and Psychopathology*, pp. 35–52. Washington, D.C.: U.S. Government Printing Office.

GARFIELD, S. L. (1948) A preliminary appraisal of Wechsler–Bellevue scatter patterns in schizophrenia. *Journal of Consulting Psychology*, **12**, 32–36.

GARFIELD, S. L. (1949) An evaluation of Wechsler-Bellevue patterns in schizophrenia. *Journal of Consulting Psychology*, **13**, 279–287.

GARFIELD, S. L., and AFFLECK, D. C. (1959) Appraisal of duration of stay in outpatient psychotherapy. *Journal of Nervous and Mental Disease*, **129**, 492–498

GARFIELD, S. L., and AFFLECK, D. C. (1961) Therapists' judgments concerning patients considered for psychotherapy. *Journal of Consulting Psychology*, **25**, 505–509.

GARFIELD, S. L., and SUNDLAND, D. M. (1966) Prognostic scales in schizophrenia. *Journal of Consulting Psychology*, **30**, 18–24.

GARMEZY, N. (1965) Process and reactive schizophrenia: Some conceptions and issues. In M. M. Katz, J. O. Cole, and W. E. Barton (Eds.), *The Role and Methodology of Classification in Psychiatry and Psychopathology*, pp. 419–466. Washington, D.C.: U.S. Government Printing Office.

GAURON, E. F., and DICKINSON, J. K. (1966a) Diagnostic decision making in psychiatry: I. Information usage. *Archives of General Psychiatry*, **14**, 225–232.

GAURON, E. F., and DICKINSON, J. K. (1966b) Diagnostic decision making in psychiatry: II. Diagnostic styles. *Archives of General Psychiatry*, **14**, 233–237.

GERTZ, B., STILSON, D. W., and GYNTHER, M. D. (1959) Reliability of the HAS as a function of length of observation and level of adjustment. *Journal of Clinical Psychology*, **15**, 36–39.

GESELL, A., GODDARD, H. H., and WALLIN, J. E. W. (1919) The field of clinical psychology as an applied science. *Journal of Applied Psychology*, **3**, 81–95.

GILHOOLY, F. M. (1950) Wechsler–Bellevue reliability and validity of certain diagnostic signs of the neuroses. *Journal of Consulting Psychology*, **14**, 82–87.

GILLESPIE, R. D. (1929) The clinical differentiation of types of depression. *Guy's Hospital Reports*, **9**, 306–344.

GILLILAND, A. R., WITTMAN, P., and GOLDMAN, M. (1945) Pattern and scatter of mental abilities in various psychoses. *Journal of General Psychology*, **29**, 251–260.

GITTELMAN-KLEIN, R. K., and KLEIN, D. F. (1969) Premorbid asocial adjustment and prognosis in schizophrenia. *Journal of Psychiatric Research*, **7**, 35–53.

GLIDEWELL, J. C., MENSH, I. N., and GILDEA, M. C. L. (1957) Behavior symptoms in children and degree of sickness. *American Journal of Psychiatry*, **114**, 47–53.

GLOVER, E. (1957) A psychoanalytic approach to the classification of mental disorders. In M. Levitt (Ed.), *Readings in Psychoanalytic Psychology*, pp. 140–161. New York: Appleton-Century-Crofts.

GOLD, L., and CHIARELLO, C. J. (1944) The prognostic value of clinical cases treated with electric shock. *Journal of Nervous and Mental Disease*, **100**, 577–583.

GOLDBERG, S. C., MATTSON, N., COLE, J. O., and KLERMAN, G. L. (1967) Prediction of improvement in schizophrenia under four phenothiazines. *Archives of General Psychiatry*, **16**, 107–117.

GOLDFARB, A. (1959) Reliability of diagnostic judgments made by psychologists. *Journal of Clinical Psychology*, **15**, 392–396.

GOLDFARB, W. (1943) A definition and validation of obsessional trends in the Rorschach examination of adolescents. *Rorschach Research Exchange*, **7**, 81–108.

GOLDFRIED, M. R., and POMERANZ, D. M. (1968) Role of assessment in behavior modification. *Psychological Reports*, **23**, 75–87.

GONDA, V. E. (1941) Treatment of mental disorders with electrically induced convulsions. *Diseases of the Nervous System*, **2**, 84–92.

GOODRICH, B. W. (1953) Quantification of the severity of every psychiatric symptom. *American Journal of Psychiatry*, **110**, 334–341.

GORHAM, D. R., and OVERALL, J. E. (1961) Dimensions of change in psychiatric symptomatology. *Diseases of the Nervous System*, **22**, 576–580.

GOSHEN, C. E. (1961) New interdisciplinary trends in psychiatry. *American Journal of Psychiatry*, **117**, 916–921.

GOUGH, H. (1971) Some reflections on the meaning of psychodiagnosis. *American Psychologist*, **26**, 160–167.

GOUGH, H. G. (1946) Diagnostic patterns on the MMPI. *Journal of Clinical Psychology*, **2**, 23–37.

GRALNICK, A. (1946) A three-year survey of electroshock therapy: Report on 276 cases; comparative value of insulin-coma therapy. *American Journal of Psychiatry*, **102**, 583–593.

GRANGER, G. W. (1961) Abnormalities of sensory perception. In H. J. Eysenck (Ed.), *Handbook of Abnormal Psychology*, pp. 108–166. New York: Basic Books.

GRANT, M. Q., IVES, V., and RANZONI, J. H. (1952) Reliability and validity of judges' ratings of adjustment on the Rorschach. *Psychological Monographs*, **66**, Whole No. 334.

GRAYSON, H. M., and TOLMAN, R. S. (1950) A semantic study of concepts of clinical psychologists and psychiatrists. *Journal of Abnormal and Social Psychology*, **45**, 216–231.

GREENBLATT, M., GROSSER, G. H., and WECHSLER, H. (1964) Differential responses of hospitalized depressed patients to somatic therapy. *American Journal of Psychiatry*, **120**, 935–943.

GRINKER, R. R., and NUNNALLY, J. C. (1965) The phenomena of depression. In M. M. Katz, J. O. Cole, and W. E. Barton (Eds.), *The Role and Methodology of Classification in Psychiatry and Psychopathology*, pp. 249–261. Washington, D.C.: U.S. Government Printing Office.

GRINKER, R. R., WERBLE, B., and DRYE, R. C. (1968) *The Borderline Syndrome: A Behavioral Study of Ego Functions*. New York: Basic Books.

GRINKER, R. R., MILLER, J., SABSHIN, M., NUNN, R., and NUNNALLY, J. (1961) *The Phenomena of Depression*. New York: Hoeber.

GROSS, H. S., HERBERT, M. R., KNATTERUD, G. L., and DONNER, L. (1969) The effect of race and sex on the variation of diagnosis and disposition in a psychiatric emergency room. *Journal of Nervous and Mental Disease*, **148**, 638–642.

GRUENBERG, E. M. (1965) Epidemiology and medical care statistics. In M. M. Katz, J. O. Cole, and W. E. Barton (Eds.), *The Role and Methodology of Classification in Psychiatry and Psychopathology*, pp. 76–97. Washington, D.C.: U.S. Government Printing Office.

GUERTIN, W. H. (1952a) A factor-analytic study of schizophrenic symptoms. *Journal of Consulting Psychology*, **16**, 308–312.

GUERTIN, W. H. (1952b) An inverted factor-analytic study of schizophrenics. *Journal of Consulting Psychology*, **16**, 371–375.

GUERTIN, W. H. (1955a) A factor analysis of schizophrenic ratings on the Hospital Adjustment Scale. *Journal of Clinical Psychology*, **11**, 70–73.

GUERTIN, W. H. (1955b) A factor analytic study of the adjustment of chronic schizophrenics. *Journal of Clinical Psychology*, **11**, 174–177.

GUERTIN, W. H. (1956a) A factor analysis of schizophrenics rated on the Activity Rating Scale. *Journal of Clinical Psychology*, **12**, 163–166.

GUERTIN, W. H. (1956b) Schizophrenics as psychiatrists diagnose them. *Psychological Reports*, **2**, 279–282.

GUERTIN, W. H. (1961) Empirical syndrome groupings of schizophrenic hospital admissions. *Journal of Clinical Psychology*, **17**, 268–275.

GUERTIN, W. H., and JENKINS, R. L. (1956) A transposed factor analysis of a group of schizophrenic patients. *Journal of Clinical Psychology*, **12**, 64–68.

GUERTIN, W. H., and KRUGMAN, A. D. (1959) A factor analytically derived scale for rating activities of psychiatric patients. *Journal of Clinical Psychology*, **15**, 32–35.

GUERTIN, W. H., and ZILAITIS, V. (1953) A transposed factor analysis of paranoid schizophrenics. *Journal of Consulting Psychology*, **17**, 455–458.

GUIRDHAM, A. (1936a) The diagnosis of depression by the Rorschach test. *British Journal of Medical Psychology*, **16**, 130–145.

GUIRDHAM, A. (1936b) Simple psychological data in melancholia. *Journal of Mental Science*, **82**, 649–653.

GUIRDHAM, A. (1937) The diagnosis of depression by the Rorschach test. *British Journal of Psychology, Medical Section*, **16**, 130–145.

GUNDERSON, E. K. E. (1965) Determinants of reliability in personality ratings. *Journal of Clinical Psychology*, **21**, 164–169.

GUNDERSON, E. K. E., and ARTHUR, R. J. (1968) Prognostic indicators in psychosis and neurosis. *Journal of Abnormal Psychology*, **73**, 468–473.

GUNDERSON, E. K. E., and KAPFER, E. L. (1966) The predictability of clinicians' evaluations from biographical data. *Journal of Clinical Psychology*, **22**, 144–150.

GUREL, L. (1967) Dimensions of psychiatric patient ward behavior. *Journal of Consulting Psychology*, **31**, 328–331.

GURLAND, B. J., FLEISS, J. L., COOPER, J. E., SHARPE, L., KENDELL, R. E., and ROBERTS, P. (1970) Cross-national study of diagnosis of mental disorders: Hospital diagnoses and hospital patients in New York and London. *Comprehensive Psychiatry*, **11**, 18–25.

GUTHRIE, G. M. (1950) Six M.M.P.I. diagnostic profile patterns. *Journal of Psychology*, **30**, 317–323.

GUTTMAN, S. A. (1960) Criteria for analyzability. *Journal of the American Psychoanalytic Association*, **8**, 141–151.

HAAS, K. (1965) Direction of hostility and psychiatric symptoms. *Psychological Reports*, **16**, 555–556.

HACKFIELD, A. W. (1935) An objective interpretation by means of the Rorschach test of the psychobiological structure underlying schizophrenia, essential hypertension, Graves' syndrome, etc. *American Journal of Psychiatry*, **92**, 575–588.

HAMILTON, D. M. (1947) The use of electric shock therapy in psychoneurosis. *American Journal of Psychiatry*, **103**, 665–668.

HAMILTON, M. (1960) A rating scale for depression. *Journal of Neurology, Neurosurgery and Psychiatry*, **23**, 56–62.

HAMILTON, M., and WHITE, J. (1959) Clinical syndromes in depressive states. *Journal of Mental Science*, **105**, 985–998.

HAMLIN, R. M., and LORR, M. (1971) Differentiation of normals, neurotics, paranoids, and nonparanoids. *Journal of Abnormal Psychology*, **77**, 90–96.

HARPER, E. A. (1950) Discrimination of the types of schizophrenia by the Wechsler–Bellevue Scale. *Journal of Consulting Psychology*, **14**, 290–296.

HARRIS, M. R., FISHER, J., and EPSTEIN, L. J. (1963) The reliability of the interview in psychiatric assessment for job placement. *Comprehensive Psychiatry*, **4**, 19–28.

HARRISON, S. I., McDERMOTT, J. F., WILSON, P. T., and SCHRAGER, J. (1965) Social class and mental illness in children. *Archives of General Psychiatry*, **13**, 411–417.

HARROW, M., TUCKER, G. J., and BROMET, E. (1969) Short-term prognosis of schizophrenic patients. *Archives of General Psychiatry*, **21**, 195–202.

HARROW, M., COLBERT, J., DETRE, T., and BAKEMAN, R. (1966) Symptomatology and subjective experience in current depressive states. *Archives of General Psychiatry*, **14**, 203–212.

HARROWER, M. (1970) Projective classification. In A. R. Maher (Ed.), *New Approaches to Personality Classification*, pp. 139–164. New York: Columbia University Press.

HARROWER-ERICKSON, M. R. (1942) The values and limitations of the so-called "neurotic signs." *Rorschach Research Exchange*, **6**, 109–114.

HATHAWAY, S. R., and MCKINLEY, J. C. (1942) A multiphasic personal schedule (Minnesota): III. The measurement of symptomatic depression. *Journal of Psychology*, **14**, 73–84.

HAUSMANN, M. F. (1933) A method to objectively demonstrate thinking difficulties. *American Journal of Psychiatry*, **13**, 613–625.

HEMPHILL, R. E., and WALTER, W. G. (1941) The treatment of mental disorders by electrically induced convulsions. *Journal of Mental Science*, **87**, 256–275.

HERRON, W. G. (1962) The process-reactive classification of schizophrenia. *Psychological Bulletin*, **59**, 329–343.

HERRON, W. G. (1963) The disease controversy: Closing open issues. *Psychological Reports*, **13**, 79–84.

HERTZ, M. R., and PAOLINO, A. F. (1960) Rorschach indices of perceptual and conceptual disorganization. *Journal of Projective Techniques*, **24**, 370–388.

HERZBERG, F. (1954) Prognostic variables for electro-shock therapy. *Journal of General Psychology*, **50**, 79–86.

HEYER, A. W. (1949) "Scatter analysis" techniques applied to anxiety neurotics from a restricted culture-educational environment. *Journal of General Psychology*, **40**, 155–166.

HILER, E. W. (1966) Prognostic indicators for children in a psychiatric hospital. *Journal of Consulting Psychology*, **30**, 169–171.

HILL, D. (1968) Depression, reaction, or posture? *American Journal of Psychiatry*, **125**, 445–457.

HIMMELWEIT, H. T., DESAI, M., and PETRIE, A. (1946) An experimental investigation of neuroticism. *Journal of Personality*, **15**, 173–196.

HIRSCH, S. J., and HOLLENDER, M. H. (1969) Hysterical psychosis: Clarification of the concept. *American Journal of Psychiatry*, **125**, 81–87.

HOCH, P. (1957) The etiology and epidemiology of schizophrenia. *American Journal of Public Health*, **47**, 1071–1076.

HOCH, P., and ZUBIN, J. (1953) (Eds.), *Current Problems in Psychiatric Diagnosis.* New York: Grune & Stratton.

HOLLENDER, M. H., and HIRSCH, S. J. (1964) Hysterical psychosis. *American Journal of Psychiatry*, **120**, 1066–1074.

HOLLINGSHEAD, A. B., and REDLICH, F. C. (1953) Social stratification and psychiatric disorders. *American Sociological Review*, **18**, 163–169.

HOLLINGSHEAD, A. B., and REDLICH, F. C. (1954) Schizophrenia and social structure. *American Journal of Psychiatry*, **110**, 695–701.

HOLLINGSHEAD, A. B., and REDLICH, F. C. (1958) *Social Class and Mental Illness: A Community Study.* New York: Wiley.

HOLSOPPLE, J. Q., and PHELAN, J. G. (1954) The skills of clinicians in analysis of projective tests. *Journal of Clinical Psychology*, **10**, 307–320.

HOLT, R. R. (1968) Editor's foreword. In D. Rapaport, M. M. Gill, and R. Schafer, *Diagnostic Psychological Testing*, pp. 1–44. New York: International Universities Press.

HOLZBERG, J. D. and DEANE, M. A. (1950) The diagnostic significance of an objective measure of intratest scatter on the Wechsler–Bellevue Intelligence Scale. *Journal of Consulting Psychology*, 14, 180–188.

HOLZBERG, J. D., and WITTENBORN, J. R. (1953) The quantified multiple diagnostic procedure in psychiatric classification. *Journal of Clinical Psychology*, 9, 145–148.

HONIGFELD, G., and KLETT, C. J. (1965) The nurse's observation scale for inpatient evaluation: A new scale for measuring improvement in chronic schizophrenia. *Journal of Clinical Psychology*, 21, 65–71.

HOOVER, K. K. (1955) An operational measurement of differential contact with reality in a normal population. Unpublished doctoral dissertation. Northwestern University.

HORN, D. (1944) A study of personality syndromes. *Character and Personality*, 12, 257–274.

HORNEY, K. (1936) Culture and neurosis. *American Sociological Review*, 1, 221–230.

HUGHES, R. M. (1950) A factor analysis of Rorschach diagnostic signs. *Journal of General Psychology*, 43, 85–103.

HUNT, J. McV. (1935) Psychological loss in paretics and schizophrenics. *American Journal of Psychology*, 47, 458–463.

HUNT, J. McV. (1936) Psychological experiments with disordered persons. *Psychological Bulletin*, 33, 1–58.

HUNT, R. C., and APPELL, K. E. (1936) Prognosis in the psychoses lying midway between schizophrenia and manic-depressive. *American Journal of Psychiatry*, 93, 313–339.

HUNT, R. C., FELDMAN, H., and FIERE, R. P. (1938) "Spontaneous" remission in dementia praecox. *Psychiatric Quarterly*, 12, 414–425.

HUNT, W. A. (1951) Clinical psychology—Science or superstition. *American Psychologist*, 6, 683–687.

HUNT, W. A., and ARNHOFF, F. N. (1955) Some standardized scales for disorganization in schizophrenic thinking. *Journal of Consulting Psychology*, 19, 171–174.

HUNT, W. A., and ARNHOFF, F. N. (1956) The repeat reliability of clinical judgments of test responses. *Journal of Clinical Psychology*, 12, 289–290.

HUNT, W. A., and JONES, N. F. (1958) The reliability of clinical judgments of asocial tendency. *Journal of Clinical Psychology*, 14, 233–235.

HUNT, W. A., and WALKER, R. E. (1962) A comparison of global and specific clinical judgments across several diagnostic categories. *Journal of Clinical Psychology*, 18, 188–194.

HUNT, W. A., ARNHOFF, F. N., and COTTON, J. W. (1954) Reliability, chance, and fantasy in inter-judge agreement among clinicians. *Journal of Clinical Psychology*, 10, 294–296.

HUNT, W. A., JONES, N. F., and HUNT, E. B. (1957) Reliability of clinical judgment as a function of clinical experience. *Journal of Clinical Psychology*, 13, 377–378.

HUNT, W. A., SCHWARTZ, M. L., and WALKER, R. E. (1965) Reliability of clinical judgments as a function of range of pathology. *Journal of Abnormal Psychology*, 70, 32–33.

HUNT, W. A., WALKER, R. E., and JONES, N. F. (1960) The validity of clinical ratings for estimating severity of schizophrenia. *Journal of Clinical Psychology*, **16**, 391–393.

HUNT, W. A., WITTSON, C. L., and HUNT, E. B. (1952) The relationship between definiteness of psychiatric diagnosis and severity of disability. *Journal of Clinical Psychology*, **8**, 314–315.

HUNT, W. A., WITTSON, C. L., and HUNT, E. B. (1953) A theoretical and practical analysis of the diagnostic process. In P. H. Hoch and J. Zubin (Eds.), *Current Problems in Psychiatric Diagnosis*, pp. 53–65. New York: Grune & Stratton.

HUNT, W. A., WITTSON, C. L., and HUNT, E. B. (1955) The relationship between amount of presenting symptomatology and severity of disability. *Journal of Clinical Psychology*, **11**, 305–306.

HYDE, R. W., and KINGSLEY, L. V. (1944) Studies in medical sociology: The relation of mental disorder to the community socioeconomic level. *New England Journal of Medicine*, **231**, 543–548.

IMBER, S. D., NASH, E. H., and STONE, A. R. (1955) Social class and duration of psychotherapy. *Journal of Clinical Psychology*, **11**, 281–284.

INGHAM, J. G., and ROBINSON, J. O. (1964) Personality in the diagnosis of hysteria. *British Journal of Psychology*, **55**, 276–284.

INGHAM, J. G., SLATER, P., SLATER, E., FOULDS, G. A., ROBINSON, J. O., and EYSENCK, H. J. (1964) Personality variables in psychiatric classification: A symposium. *British Journal of Psychology*, **55**, 253–294.

ITTELSON, W. H., SEIDENBERG, B., and KUTASH, S. B. (1961) Some perceptual differences in somatizing and nonsomatizing neuropsychiatric patients. *Psychosomatic Medicine*, **23**, 219–223.

JACKSON, B. (1970) The revised diagnostic and statistical manual of the American Psychiatric Association. *American Journal of Psychiatry*, **127**, 65–73.

JACKSON, C. L., and JACO, E. G. (1954) Some prognostic factors in 538 transorbital lobotomy cases. *American Journal of Psychiatry*, **111**, 353–357.

JENKINS, R. L. (1953) Symptomatology and dynamics in diagnosis: A medical perspective. *Journal of Clinical Psychology*, **9**, 149–150.

JENKINS, R. L., and GUREL, L. (1959) Predictive factors in early release. *Mental Hospital*, **10**, 11–14.

JENKINS, R. L., and HEWITT, L. (1944) Types of personality structure encountered in child guidance clinics. *American Journal of Orthopsychiatry*, **14**, 84–94.

JENKINS, R. L., and LORR, M. (1954) Type-tracking among psychotic patients. *Journal of Clinical Psychology*, **10**, 114–119.

JENKINS, R. L., STAUFFACHER, J., and HESTER, R. A. (1959) A symptom rating scale for use with psychotic patients. *Archives of General Psychiatry*, **1**, 197–204.

JOHANNSEN, W. J. (1964) On classifying schizophrenics: A modest proposal. *Psychological Reports*, **14**, 38.

JOHANNSEN, W. J., FRIEDMAN, S. H., LEISCHUH, T. H., and AMMONS, H. (1963) A study of certain schizophrenic dimensions and their relationship to double alternation learning. *Journal of Consulting Psychology*, **27**, 375–382.

JOHNSON, L. C. (1949) Wechsler–Bellevue pattern analysis in schizophrenia. *Journal of Consulting Psychology*, **13**, 32–33.

JONES, N. F. (1957) Context effects in judgment as a function of experience. *Journal of Clinical Psychology*, **13**, 379–382.

JONES, N. F. (1959) The validity of clinical judgments of schizophrenic pathology based on verbal responses to intelligence test items. *Journal of Clinical Psychology*, **15**, 396–400.

JONES, N. F., KAHN, M. W., and LANGSLEY, D. G. (1965) Prediction of admission to a psychiatric hospital. *Archives of General Psychiatry*, **12**, 607–610.

JUNG, C. G. (1923) *Psychological Types*. London: Kegan Paul.

KAHN, E., and POKORNY, A. D. (1964) Concerning the concept of schizophrenia. *American Journal of Psychiatry*, **120**, 856–860.

KAHN, J. H. (1969) Dimensions of diagnosis and treatment. *Mental Hygiene*, **53**, 229–236.

KAHN, R. L., and FINK, M. (1959) Personality factors in behavioral responses to electroshock therapy. *Journal of Neuropsychiatry*, **1**, 45–49.

KAHN, R. L., FINK, M., and SIEGEL, N. (1966) Sociopsychological aspects of psychiatric treatment. *Archives of General Psychiatry*, **14**, 20–25.

KALINOWSKY, L. B. and BARRERA, E. S. (1940) Electric convulsion therapy in mental disorders. *Psychiatric Quarterly*, **14**, 719–730.

KALINOWSKY, L. B., and WORTHING, H. J. (1943) Results with electric convulsive therapy in 200 cases of schizophrenia. *Psychiatric Quarterly*, **17**, 144–153.

KALINOWSKY, L. B., BIGELOW, N., and BRIKATES, P. (1941) Electric shock therapy in a state hospital practice. *Psychiatric Quarterly*, **15**, 450–459.

KANFER, F. H., and SASLOW, G. (1965) Behavioral analysis: An alternative to diagnostic classification. *Archives of General Psychiatry*, **12**, 529–538.

KANNER, L. (1943) Autistic disturbances of affective contact. *Nervous Child*, **2**, 217–250.

KANNER, L. (1949) Problems of nosology and psychodynamics of early infantile autism. *American Journal of Orthopsychiatry*, **19**, 416–426.

KANT, I. (1964) *The Classification of Mental Disorders*. Doylestown, Penn.: Doylestown Fund.

KANT, O. (1940a) Differential diagnosis of schizophrenia in light of concept of personality stratification. *American Journal of Psychiatry*, **97**, 342–357.

KANT, O. (1940b) Types and analysis of the clinical pictures of recovered schizophrenics. *Psychiatric Quarterly*, **14**, 676–700.

KANT, O. (1941a) The relation of a group of highly-improved schizophrenic patients to one group of completely-recovered and another group of deteriorated patients. *Psychiatric Quarterly*, **15**, 779–789.

KANT, O. (1941b) A comparative study of recovered and deteriorated schizophrenic patients. *Journal of Nervous and Mental Disease*, **93**, 616–624.

KANT, O. (1944) Evaluation of prognostic criteria in schizophrenia. *Journal of Nervous and Mental Disease*, **100**, 598–605.

KANTOR, R. N., and HERRON, W. G. (1966) *Reactive and Process Schizophrenia*. Palo Alto, Calif.: Science & Behavior Books.

KARNO, M. (1966) The enigma of ethnicity in a psychiatric clinic. *Archives of General Psychiatry*, **14**, 516–520.

KARUSH, A., EASSER, B. R., COOPER, A., and SWERDLOFF, B. (1964) The evaluation of ego strength I: A profile of adaptive balance. *Journal of Nervous and Mental Disease*, **139**, 332–349.

KASANIN, J. (1933) Acute schizoaffective psychoses. *American Journal of Psychiatry*, **13**, 97–126.

KASANIN, J., and KAUFMAN, M. R. (1929) A study of functional psychoses in childhood. *American Journal of Psychiatry*, **9**, 307–384.

KATAGUCHI, Y. (1959) Rorschach Schizophrenic Score (RSS). *Journal of Projective Techniques*, **23**, 214–222.

KATZ, M. M. (1965) A phenomenological typology of schizophrenia. In M. M. Katz, J. O. Cole, and W. E. Barton (Eds.), *The Role and Methdology of Classification in Psychiatry and Psychopathology*, pp. 300–322. Washington, D.C.: U.S. Government Printing Office.

KATZ, M. M., and COLE, J. O. (1963) A phenomenological approach to the classification of schizophrenic disorders. *Diseases of the Nervous System*, **24**, 147–154.

KATZ, M. M., and LYERLY, S. B. (1963) Methods for measuring adjustment and social behavior in the community: I. Rationale, description, discriminative validity and scale development. *Psychological Reports, Monographs*, **13**, 503–535.

KATZ, M. M., COLE, J. O., and BARTON, W. E. (1965) (Eds.), *The Role and Methodology of Classification in Psychiatry and Psychopathology*. Washington, D.C.: U.S. Government Printing Office.

KATZ, M. M., COLE, J. O., and LOWERY, H. A. (1964) The nonspecificity of the diagnosis of paranoid schizophrenia. *Archives of General Psychiatry*, **11**, 197–202.

KATZ, M. M., COLE, J. O., and LOWERY, H. A. (1969) Studies on the diagnostic process: The influence of symptom perception, past experience, and ethnic background on diagnostic decisions. *American Journal of Psychiatry*, **125**, 937–947.

KATZENBOGEN, S., HARMS, H. E., WILLIAMS, R., BARKOFF, S., BRODY, M. W., and HAYMAN, M. (1939) The insulin treatment in schizophrenic patients. *American Journal of Psychiatry*, **5**, 794–797.

KAY, D. W. K., GARSIDE, R. F., BEAMISH, P., and ROY, J. R. (1969) Endogenous and neurotic syndromes of depression: A factor analytic study of 104 cases. *British Journal of Psychiatry*, **115**, 377–388.

KELLEY, D. M., and KLOPFER, B. (1939) Application of the Rorschach method to research in schizophrenia. *Rorschach Research Exchange*, **3**, 55–66.

KEMPF, E. J. (1915) The behavior chart in mental disease. *American Journal of Insanity*, **71**, 761–772.

KENDELL, R. E., COOPER, J. E., GOURLAY, A. J., COPELAND, J. R. M., SHARPE, L., and GURLAND, B. J. (1971) Diagnostic criteria of American and British psychiatrists. *Archives of General Psychiatry*, **25**, 123–130.

KETY, S. S. (1965) Problems in psychiatric nosology from the viewpoint of the biological sciences. In M. M. Katz, J. O. Cole, and W. E. Barton (Eds.), *The Role of Methodology of Classification in Psychiatry and Psychopathology*, pp. 190–193. Washington, D.C.: U.S. Government Printing Office.

KILOH, G., and GARSIDE, R. F. (1963) The independence of neurotic depression and endogenous depression. *British Journal of Psychiatry*, **109**, 451–453.

KILOH, L. G., BALL, J. R., and GARSIDE, R. F. (1962) Prognostic factors in treatment of depressive states with imipramine. *British Medical Journal*, **1**, 1225–1227.

KLAF, F. S., and HAMILTON, J. G. (1961) Schizophrenia: A hundred years ago and today. *Journal of Mental Science*, **107**, 819–827.

KLEHR, H. (1949) Clinical intuition and test scores as a basis for diagnosis. *Journal of Consulting Psychology*, **13**, 34–38.

KLEIN, D. F. (1967) Importance of psychiatric diagnosis in prediction of clinical drug effects. *Archives of General Psychiatry*, **16**, 118–126.

KLEIN, G. S. (1948) An application of the multiple regression principle to clinical prediction. *Journal of General Psychology*, **38**, 159–179.

KLEINMUTH, B. (1960) Two types of paranoid schizophrenia. *Journal of Clinical Psychology*, **16**, 310–312.

KLERMAN, G. L., and PAYKEL, E. S. (1970) Depressive patterns, social background, and hospitalization. *Journal of Nervous and Mental Disease*, **150**, 466–478.

KLETT, C. J., and MOSELY, E. L. (1965) The right drug for the right patient. *Journal of Consulting Psychology*, **29**, 546–551.

KLINGER, E., and ROTH, I. (1964) Diagnosing schizophrenia with Rorschach color responses. *Journal of Clinical Psychology*, **20**, 386–388.

KLINGER, E., and ROTH, I. (1965) Diagnosis of schizophrenia by Rorschach patterns. *Journal of Projective Techniques and Personality Assessment*, **29**, 323–335.

KNAPP, P. H., LEVIN, S., MCCARTER, R. H., WERMER, H., and ZETZEL, E. (1960) Suitability for psychoanalysis: A review of one hundred supervised analytic cases. *Psychoanalytic Quarterly*, **29**, 459–477.

KNOFF, W. F. (1970) A history of the concept of neurosis, with a memoir of William Cullen. *American Journal of Psychiatry*, **127**, 80–84.

KNOPF, I. J. (1956) Rorschach summary scores in differential diagnosis. *Journal of Consulting Psychology*, **20**, 99–104.

KOBLER, F. J., and STIEL, A. (1953) The use of the Rorschach in involutional melancholia. *Journal of Consulting Psychology*, **17**, 365–370.

KOGAN, W. S. (1950) An investigation into the relationship between psychometric pattern and psychiatric diagnosis. *Journal of General Psychology*, **43**, 17–46.

KOLB, L., and VOGEL, V. H. (1942) The use of shock therapy in 305 mental hospitals. *American Journal of Psychiatry*, **99**, 90–100.

KOSTLAN, A. (1954) A method for the empirical study of psychodiagnosis. *Journal of Consulting Psychology*, **18**, 83–88.

KRAEPLIN, E. (1902) *Clinical Psychiatry*. New York: Macmillan.

KRAEPLIN, E. (1921) *Manic-depressive Insanity and Paranoia*. Edinburgh: E. & S. Livingstone.

KRAUS, J. (1965) Psychiatric evaluation and differential value of WAIS subtest scores. *Australian Journal of Psychology*, **17**, 137–139.

KREITMAN, N. (1961) The reliability of psychiatric diagnosis. *Journal of Mental Science*, **107**, 876–886.

KREITMAN, N., SAINSBURY, P., MORRISSEY, J., and SCRIVNER, J. (1961) The reliability of psychiatric assessment: An analysis. *Journal of Mental Science*, **107**, 887–908.

LANGFELDT, G. (1937) The prognosis in schizophrenia and the factors influencing the course of the disease. *Acta Psychiatrica, Supplement*, 1–228.

LANGFELDT, G. (1953) The importance of constitution in psychiatry. *American Journal of Psychiatry*, **110**, 361–368.

LANGFELDT, G. (1959) The significance of a dichotomy in clinical psychiatric classification. *American Journal of Psychiatry*, **116**, 537–539.

LANGFORD, W. S. (1964) Reflections on classification in child psychiatry as related to the activities of the Committee on Child Psychiatry of the Group for the Advancement of Psychiatry. In R. L. Jenkins and J. O. Cole (Eds.), *Diagnostic Classification in Child Psychiatry*, pp. 1–15. Washington, D.C.: American Psychiatric Association.

LANZKRON, J. and WOLFSON, W. (1958) Prognostic value of perception distortion of temporal orientation in chronic schizophrenics. *American Journal of Psychiatry*, **114**, 744–746.

LAZARE, A. (1971) The hysterical character in psychoanalytic theory: Evolution and confusion. *Archives of General Psychiatry*, **25**, 131–137.

LEARY, T. (1970) The diagnosis of behavior and the diagnosis of experience. In A. R. Mahrer (Ed.), *New Approaches to Personality Classification*, pp. 211–236. New York: Columbia University Press.

LEARY, T., and COFFEY, H. (1955) Interpersonal diagnosis: Some problems of methodology and validation. *Journal of Abnormal and Social Psychology*, **50**, 110–126.

LEHRMAN, N. S. (1960) A state hospital population five years after admission: A yardstick for evaluative comparison of follow-up studies. *Psychiatric Quarterly*, **34**, 658–681.

LESSE, S. (1968) The multivariate mask of depression. *American Journal of Psychiatry*, **124**, May Supplement, 35–40.

LEVIN, H. L. (1931) Recovery in dementia praecox. *Psychiatric Quarterly*, **5**, 476–491.

LEVINE, D., and COHEN, J. (1962) Symptoms and ego strength measures as predictors of the outcome of hospitalization in functional psychoses. *Journal of Consulting Psychology*, **26**, 246–250.

LEVINE, D., and WITTENBORN, J. R. (1970) Relation of expressed attitudes to improvement in functional psychotics. *Psychological Reports*, **26**, 275–277.

LEVINE, L. S. (1949) The utility of Wechsler's patterns in the diagnosis of schizophrenia. *Journal of Consulting Psychology*, **13**, 28–31.

LEVY, D. M., and BECK, S. J. (1934) The Rorschach test in manic-depressive psychosis. *American Journal of Orthopsychiatry*, **4**, 31–42.

LEVY, M. R., and KAHN, M. W. (1970) Interpreter bias on the Rorschach test as a function of patients' socioeconomic status. *Journal of Projective Techniques and Personality Assessment*, **34**, 106–112.

LEWIN, K. (1931) The conflict between Aristotelian and Galilean modes of thought in contemporary psychology. *Journal of General Psychology*, **5**, 141–177.

LEWINSKI, R. J. (1945) The psychometric pattern: I. Anxiety neurosis. *Journal of Clinical Psychology*, **1**, 214–221.

LEWINSOHN, P. M. (1967) Factors related to improvement in mental hospital patients. *Journal of Consulting Psychology*, **31**, 588–594.

LEWIS, A. J. (1934) Melancholia: Clinical survey of depressive states. *Journal of Mental Science*, **80**, 277–378.

LEWIS, A. J. (1936) Problems of obsessional illness. *Proceedings of the Royal Society of Medicine*, **29**, 325–336.

LEWIS, A. J. (1938) States of depression: Their clinical and aetiological differentiation. *British Medical Journal*, **2**, 875–878.

LEWIS, N. D. C., and BLANCHARD, E. (1931) Clinical findings in recovered cases of schizophrenia. *American Journal of Psychiatry*, **11**, 481–492.

LEWIS, N. D. C., and PIOTROWSKI, Z. A. (1954) Clinical diagnosis of manic-depressive psychosis. In P. H. Hoch and J. Zubin (Eds.), *Depression*, pp. 25–38. New York: Grune & Stratton.

LIBERTSON, W. (1941) Critical analysis of insulin therapy at Rochester State Hospital. *Psychiatric Quarterly*, **15**, 635–647.

LIEF, H. I., LIEF, V. F., WARREN, C. O., and HEATH, R. G. (1961) Low drop-out rate in psychiatric clinic. *Archives of General Psychiatry*, **5**, 200–211.

LINDEMANN, J. E., FAIRWEATHER, G. W., STONE, G. B., and SMITH, R. S. (1959) The use of demographic characteristics in predicting length of neuropsychiatric stay. *Journal of Consulting Psychology*, **23**, 85–89.

LINN, E. L. (1962) The relation of chronicity in the functional psychoses to prognosis. *Journal of Nervous and Mental Disease*, **135**, 460–467.

LIPKIN, K. M., DYRUD, J., and MEYER, C. G. (1970) The many faces of mania. *Archives of General Psychiatry*, **22**, 262–267.

LIPMAN, R. S., RICKELS, K., COVI, L., DEROGATIS, L. R., and UHLENHUTH, E. H. (1969) Dimensions of symptom distress in doctor ratings of anxious neurotic outpatients. *Archives of General Psychiatry*, **21**, 328–338.

LIPSCHUTZ, Z. S., CAVELL, R. W., LEISER, R., HINKS, E. W., and RUSKIN, S. H. (1939) Evaluation of therapeutic factors in pharmacological shock. *American Journal of Psychiatry*, **96**, 347–360.

LORD, J. R., and FLEMING, G. W. T. H. (1932) The revision of the classification of mental disorders. Part I. *Journal of Mental Science*, **78**, 177–201.

LORR, M. (1953a) Multidimensional Scale for Rating Psychotic Patients. *Veterans Administration Technical Bulletin*, **10**, 507.

LORR, M. (1953b) The classification problem in psychopathology. *Journal of Clinical Psychology*, **9**, 143–144.

LORR, M. (1957) The Wittenborn psychiatric syndromes: An oblique rotation. *Journal of Consulting Psychology*, **21**, 439–444.

LORR, M. (1965) A typology for functional psychotics. In M. M. Katz, J. O. Cole, and W. E. Barton (Eds.), *The Role and Methodology of Classification in Psychiatry and Psychopathology*, pp. 261–277. Washington, D.C.: U.S. Government Printing Office.

LORR, M. (1966) (Ed.), *Explorations in Typing Psychotics*. London: Pergamon Press.

LORR, M. (1970) A typological conception of the behavior disorders. In A. R. Mahrer (Ed.), *New Approaches to Personality Classification*, pp. 101–116. New York: Columbia University Press.

LORR, M., and CAVE, R. (1966) The equivalence of psychotic syndromes across two media. *Multivariate Behavioral Research*, **1**, 189–195.

LORR, M., and HAMLIN, R. M. (1971) A multimethod factor analysis of behavioral and objective measures of psychopathology. *Journal of Consulting and Clinical Psychology*, **36**, 136–141.

LORR, M., and JENKINS, R. L. (1957) Patterns of maladjustment in children. *Journal of Clinical Psychology*, **9**, 16–19.

LORR, M., and KLETT, C. J. (1965) The constancy of psychotic syndromes in men and women. *Journal of Consulting Psychology*, **29**, 309–313.

LORR, M., and MCNAIR, D. M. (1963) An interpersonal behavior circle. *Journal of Abnormal and Social Psychology*, **67**, 68–75.

LORR, M., and O'CONNOR, J. P. (1962) Psychotic symptom patterns in a behavior inventory. *Educational and Psychological Measurement*, **22**, 139–146.

LORR, M., and RUBINSTEIN, E. A. (1955) Factors descriptive of psychiatric outpatients. *Journal of Abnormal and Social Psychology*, **51**, 514–522.

LORR, M., and RUBINSTEIN, E. A. (1956) Personality patterns of neurotic adults in psychotherapy. *Journal of Consulting Psychology*, **20**, 257–263.

LORR, M., and VESTRE, N. D. (1969) The psychotic inpatient profile: A nurse's observation scale. *Journal of Clinical Psychology*, **25**, 137–140.

LORR, M., BISHOP, P. F., and MCNAIR, D. M. (1965) Interpersonal types among psychiatric patients. *Journal of Abnormal Psychology*, **70**, 468–472.

LORR, M., CAFFEY, E. M., and GESSNER, T. L. (1968) Seven symptom profiles. *Journal of Nervous and Mental Disease*, **147**, 134–140.

LORR, M., JENKINS, R. L., and O'CONNOR, J. P. (1955) Factors descriptive of psychopathology and behavior of hospitalized psychotics. *Journal of Abnormal and Social Psychology*, **50**, 78–86.

LORR, M., KATZ, M. M., and RUBINSTEIN, E. A. (1958) Prediction of length of stay in psychotherapy. *Journal of Consulting Psychology*, **22**, 321–327.

LORR, M., KLETT, C. J., and CAVE, R. (1967) Higher level psychotic syndromes. *Journal of Abnormal Psychology*, **72**, 74–77.

LORR, M., KLETT, C. J., and MCNAIR, D. M. (1963) *Syndromes of Psychosis*. New York: Macmillan.

LORR, M., KLETT, C. J., and MCNAIR, D. M. (1964) Ward-observable psychotic behavior syndromes. *Educational and Psychological Measurement*, **24**, 291–300.

LORR, M., O'CONNOR, J. P., and STAFFORD, J. W. (1957) Confirmation of nine psychotic symptom patterns. *Journal of Clinical Psychology*, **13**, 252–257.

LORR, M., O'CONNOR, J. P., and STAFFORD, J. W. (1960) The psychotic reaction profile. *Journal of Clinical Psychology*, **16**, 241–245.

LORR, M., RUBINSTEIN, E. A., and JENKINS, R. L. (1953) A factor analysis of personality ratings of outpatients in psychotherapy. *Journal of Abnormal and Social Psychology*, **48**, 511–514.

LORR, M., SONN, T. M., and KATZ, M. M. (1967) Toward a definition of depression. *Archives of General Psychiatry*, **17**, 183–186.

LORR, M., WITTMAN, P., and SCHANBERGER, W. (1951) An analysis of the Elgin prognostic scale. *Journal of Clinical Psychology*, **7**, 260–263.

LORR, M., MCNAIR, D. M., KLETT, C. J., and LASKY, J. J. (1962) Evidence of ten psychotic syndromes. *Journal of Consulting Psychology*, **26**, 185–189.

LORR, M., SCHAEFER, E., RUBINSTEIN, E. A., and JENKINS, R. L. (1953) An analysis of an outpatient ratings scale. *Journal of Clinical Psychology*, **9**, 296–299.

LOW, A. A., SONENTHAL, I. R., BALUROCK, M. F., KAPLAN, M., and SHERMAN, L. (1938) Metrazol shock treatment of the "functional" psychoses. *Archives of Neurology and Psychiatry*, **39**, 717–736.

LUBIN, A. (1970) Some contributions to the testing of psychological hypotheses by means of statistical multivariate analysis. Unpublished doctoral dissertation, University of London, 1951. Referred to in H. J. Eysenck, A dimensional system of psychodiagnosis. In A. R. Mahrer (Ed.), *New Approaches to Personality Classification*, pp. 169–207. New York: Columbia University Press.

LUBIN, B. (1965) Adjective check list for measurement of depression. *Archives of General Psychiatry*, **12**, 57–62.

LUBIN, B. (1966) Fourteen brief depression adjective checklists. *Archives of General Psychiatry*, **15**, 205–208.

LUCERO, R. J., and MEYER, B. T. (1951) A behavior rating scale suitable for use in mental hospitals. *Journal of Clinical Psychology*, **7**, 250–254.

LYLE, J. G. (1956) Obsessive–compulsive behavior: Problems of Rorschach diagnosis and classification. *British Journal of Medical Psychology*, **29**, 280–286.

MACKINNON, D. W. (1949) Psychodiagnosis in clinical practice and personality theory. *Journal of Abnormal and Social Psychology*, **44**, 7–13.

MAGARET, A. (1942) Parallels in the behavior of schizophrenic, paretics and presenile non-psychotic patients. *Journal of Abnormal and Social Psychology*, **37**, 511–528.

MAGARET, A., and WRIGHT, C. (1943) Limitations in the use of intelligence test performance to detect mental disturbance. *Journal of Applied Psychology*, **27**, 387–398.

MAHRER, A. R. (1970a) (Ed.), *New Approaches to Personality Classification*. New York: Columbia University Press.

MAHRER, A. R. (1970b) Motivational theory: Foundations of personality. In *New Approaches to Personality Classification*, pp. 239–276. New York: Columbia University Press.

MAHRER, A. R. (1970c) Motivational theory: A system of personality classification. In *New Approaches to Personality Classification*, pp. 277–307. New York: Columbia University Press.

MAHRER, A. R. (1970d) Present trends and future directions. In *New Approaches to Personality Classification*, pp. 397–413. New York: Columbia University Press.

MAHRER, A. R., and BERNSTEIN, R. (1969) Depression: Characteristic syndromes and a prefatory conceptualization. *Journal of General Psychology*, **81**, 217–229.

MALAMUD, W., and MALAMUD, I. (1943) A socio-psychiatric investigation of schizophrenia occurring in the armed forces. *Psychosomatic Medicine*, **5**, 364–375.

MALAMUD, W., and RENDER, N. (1939) Course and prognosis in schizophrenia. *American Journal of Psychiatry*, **95**, 1039–1057.

MALAMUD, W., HOAGLAND, H., and KAUFMAN, I. C. (1946) A new psychiatric rating scale. *Psychosomatic Medicine*, **8**, 243–245.

MALLET, B. L., and GOLD, S. (1964) A pseudoschizophrenic hysterical syndrome. *British Journal of Medical Psychology*, **37**, 59–70.

MALZBERG, B. (1938) Outcome of insulin treatment of one thousand patients with dementia praecox. *Psychiatric Quarterly*, **12**, 528–553.

MALZBERG, B. (1939) A follow-up study of patients with dementia praecox treated with insulin in the New York civil state hospitals. *Mental Hygiene*, **23**, 641–651.

MALZBERG, B. (1943) Electro shock therapy: Outcome in New York civil state hospitals. *Psychiatric Quarterly*, **17**, 154–163.

MARKS, J., STAUFFACHER, J. C., and LYLE, C. (1963) Predicting outcome in schizophrenia. *Journal of Abnormal and Social Psychology*, **66**, 117–127.

MARKS, J., STAUFFACHER, J. C., DIAMOND, L. S., and AX, A. F. (1960) Physiological reactions and psychiatric prognosis. *Journal of Nervous and Mental Disease*, **130**, 217–223.

MARMOR, J. (1953) Orality in the hysterical personality. *Journal of the American Psychoanalytic Association*, **1**, 656–671.

MARZOLF, S. S. (1945) Symptom and syndrome statistically interpreted. *Psychological Bulletin*, **42**, 162–176.

MASLOW, A. H. (1948) Cognition of the particular and of the generic. *Psychological Review*, **55**, 22–40.

MASON, A. S., TARPY, E. K., SHERMAN, L. J., and HAEFNER, D. P. (1960) Discharges from a mental hospital in relation to social class and other variables. *Archives of General Psychiatry*, **2**, 1–6.

MASSERMAN, J. H., and CARMICHAEL, H. T. (1938) Diagnosis and prognosis in psychiatry: with a follow-up study of the results of short-term general hospital therapy of psychiatric cases. *Journal of Mental Science*, **84**, 893–946.

MASTERSON, J. F. (1956) Prognoses in adolescent disorders: Schizophrenia. *Journal of Nervous and Mental Disease*, **124**, 219–232.

MASTERSON, J. F. (1958) Prognosis in adolescent disorders. *American Journal of Psychiatry*, **114**, 1097–1103.

MAY, R. (1971) Psychotherapy and the daimonic. In A. H. Mahrer and L. Parsons (Eds.), *Creative Developments in Psychotherapy*, pp. 166–179. Cleveland: Case Western Reserve University Press.

McCONAGHY, N., JOFFE, A. D., and MURPHY, B. (1967) The independence of neurotic and endogenous depression. *British Journal of Psychiatry*, **113**, 479–484.

McDERMOTT, J. F., HARRISON, S. I., SCHRAGER, J., and WILSON, P. (1965) Social class and mental illness in children: Observations of blue-collar families. *American Journal of Orthopsychiatry*, **35**, 500–508.

McDERMOTT, J. F., HARRISON, S. I., SCHRAGER, J., LINDY, J., and KILLINS, E. (1967) Social class and mental illness in children: The question of childhood psychosis. *American Journal of Orthopsychiatry*, **37**, 548–557.

McKEEVER, W. F., and MAY, P. R. A. (1964) The MACC Scale as a predictor of length of hospitalization for schizophrenic patients: A cross validation. *Journal of Consulting Psychology*, **28**, 474.

McKENDREE, O. J. (1942) Insulin follow-up study of 87 cases 1 to 4 years after treatment with hypoglycemic therapy. *Psychiatric Quarterly*, **16**, 572–577.

McKINLEY, J. C., and HATHAWAY, S. R. (1940) A multiphasic personality schedule (Minnesota): II. A differential study of hypochondriasis. *Journal of Psychology*, **10**, 255–268.

McKINLEY, J. C., and HATHAWAY, S. R. (1942) A multiphasic personality schedule (Minnesota): IV. Psychasthenia. *Journal of Applied Psychology*, **26**, 614–624.

McKINLEY, J. C., and HATHAWAY, S. R. (1944) The Minnesota Multiphasic Personality Inventory. V. Hysteria, hypomania, and psychopathic deviate. *Journal of Applied Psychology*, **28**, 153–174.

McNAIR, D. M., and LORR, M. (1965) Differential typing of psychiatric outpatients. *Psychological Record*, **15**, 33–41.

McREYNOLDS, P. (1951) Perception of Rorschach concepts as related to personality deviation. *Journal of Abnormal and Social Psychology*, **46**, 131–141.

MEADOW, A., and STOKER, D. (1965) Symptomatic behavior of hospitalized patients: A study of Mexican American and Anglo-American patients. *Archives of General Psychiatry*, **12**, 267–277.

MEEHL, P. E. (1946) Profile analysis of the MMPI in differential diagnosis. *Journal of Applied Psychology*, **30**, 517–524.

MEEHL, P. E. (1954) *Clinical vs. Statistical Prediction*. Minneapolis: University of Minnesota Press.

MEEHL, P. E. (1956) Wanted—a good cookbook. *American Psychologist*, **11**, 262–272.

MEEHL, P. E. (1959) A comparison of clinicians with five statistical methods of identifying psychotic MMPI profiles. *Journal of Consulting Psychology*, **50**, 87–92.

MEEHL, P. E. (1960) The cognitive activity of the clinician. *American Psychologist*, **15**, 19–27.

MEEHL, P. E., and DAHLSTROM, W. G. (1960) Objective configurational rules for discriminating psychotic from neurotic MMPI profiles. *Journal of Consulting Psychology*, **24**, 375–387.

MEHLMAN, B. (1952) The reliability of psychiatric diagnosis. *Journal of Abnormal and Social Psychology*, **47**, 577–578.

MELDMAN, M. J. (1964) A nosology of the attentional diseases. *American Journal of Psychiatry*, **121**, 377–379.

MELGES, F. T., and BOWLBY, J. (1969) Types of hopelessness in psychopathological process. *Archives of General Psychiatry*, **20**, 690–699.

MENDEL, W. M. (1966) Effects of length of hospitalization on rate and quality of remission from acute psychotic episodes. *Journal of Nervous and Mental Disease*, **143**, 226–233.

MENDEL, W. M., and RAPPORT, S. (1969) Determinants of the decision for psychiatric hospitalization. *Archives of General Psychiatry*, **20**, 321–328.

MENDELS, J. (1965) Electroconvulsive therapy and depression: II. Significance of endogenous and reactive syndromes. *British Journal of Psychiatry*, **111**, 682–686.

MENDELS, J. (1968) Depression: The distinction between syndrome and symptom. *British Journal of Psychiatry*, **114**, 1549–1554.

MENDELS, J., and COCHRANE, C. (1968) The nosology of depression: The endogenous-reactive concept. *American Journal of Psychiatry*, **124**, May Supplement, 1–11.

MENNINGER, K. A. (1954a) Regulatory devices of the ego under major stress. *International Journal of Psychoanalysis*, **35**, 412–430.

MENNINGER, K. A. (1954b) Psychological aspects of the organism under stress. Part I. The homeostatic regulatory function of the ego. *Journal of the American Psychoanalytic Association*, **2**, 67–106.

MENNINGER, K. A. (1954c) Psychological aspects of the organism under stress. Part II. Regulatory devices of the ego under major stress. *Journal of the American Psychoanalytic Association*, **2**, 280–310.

MENNINGER, K. A. (1959a) The psychological examination in the psychiatric case study. *Bulletin of the Menninger Clinic*, **23**, 131–143.

MENNINGER, K. A. (1959b) The psychiatric diagnosis. *Bulletin of the Menninger Clinic*, **23**, 226–243.

MENNINGER, K., MAYMAN, M., and PRUYSER, P. (1963) *The Vital Balance*. New York: Viking Press.

MENNINGER, K., ELLENBERGER, H., PRUYSER, P., and MAYMAN, M. (1958) The unitary concept of mental illness. *Bulletin of the Menninger Clinic*, **22**, 4–12.

MENSH, I. N., and MATARAZZO, J. D. (1954) Rorschach card rejection in psychodiagnosis. *Journal of Consulting Psychology*, **18**, 271–275.

MERCER, M. (1949) Diagnostic testing in two cases of schizophrenic depression. *Journal of Psychology*, **28**, 147–160.

MEYER, A. (1903) An attempt at analysis of the neurotic constitution. *American Journal of Psychology*, **14**, 90–103.

MEYER, A. (1912) Pathopsychology and psychopathology. *Psychological Bulletin*, 9, 129–145.

MEYER, A. (1917) The aims and meaning of psychiatric diagnosis. *American Journal of Insanity*, 74, 163–168.

MEYER, A. (1951a) A review of recent problems of psychiatry (1904). In *The Collected Papers of Adolf Meyer*, Vol. II, pp. 331–385. Baltimore: The Johns Hopkins Press.

MEYER, A. (1951b) Genetic-dynamic psychology versus nosology (1926). In *The Collected Papers of Adolf Meyer*, Vol. III, pp. 57–73. Baltimore: The Johns Hopkins Press.

MIALE, F. R., and HARROWER-ERICKSON, M. R. (1940) Personality structure in the psychoneuroses. *Rorschach Research Exchange*, 4, 71–74.

MICHAEL, S. T. (1967) Social class and psychiatric treatment. *Journal of Psychiatric Research*, 5, 243–254.

MICHAELS, J. J. (1959) Character disorders and acting upon impulse. In M. Levitt (Ed.), *Readings in Psychoanalytic Psychology*, pp. 181–196. New York: Appleton-Century-Crofts.

MILLER, C. W. (1939) Shock therapy in schizophrenia. *American Journal of Psychiatry*, 95, 808–811.

MILLER, L. C. (1964) Q-sort agreement among observers of children. *American Journal of Orthopsychiatry*, 34, 71–75.

MOLISH, H. B. (1951) The popular responses in Rorschach records of normals, neurotics, and schizophrenics. *American Journal of Orthopsychiatry*, 21, 523–531.

MOLISH, H. B., and BECK, S. J. (1958a) Further explorations of the "six schizophrenias": Type S-3. *American Journal of Orthopsychiatry*, 28, 483–505.

MOLISH, H. B., and BECK, S. J. (1958b) Further exploration of the "six schizophrenias": Type S-3. *American Journal of Orthopsychiatry*, 28, 809–827.

MONRO, A. B. (1954) A rating scale developed for use in clinical psychiatric investigations. *Journal of Mental Science*, 100, 657–669.

MONRO, A. B. (1955) Psychiatric types: A Q-technique study of 200 patients. *Journal of Mental Science*, 101, 330–343.

MONTAGU, A. (1955) *The Direction of Human Development*. New York: Hawthorne Books.

MONTAGU, A. (1961) Culture and mental illness. *American Journal of Psychiatry*, 118, 15–23.

MOORE, R. A., BENEDEK, E. P., and WALLACE, J. G. (1963) Social class, schizophrenia and the psychiatrist. *American Journal of Psychiatry*, 120, 149–154.

MOORE, T. V. (1930) The empirical determination of certain syndromes underlying praecox and manic-depressive psychoses. *American Journal of Psychiatry*, 86, 719–738.

MORAN, L. J., MORAN, F. A., and BLAKE, R. R. (1952a) An investigation of the vocabulary performance of schizophrenics: I. Quantitative level. *Journal of Genetic Psychology*, 80, 97–100.

MORAN, L. J., MORAN, F. A., and BLAKE, R. R. (1952b) An investigation of the vocabulary performance of schizophrenics: II. Conceptual level definitions. *Journal of Genetic Psychology*, 80, 107–132.

MORAN, L. J., FAIRWEATHER, G. W., MORTON, R. B., and McGAUGHRAN, L. S. (1955) The use of demographic characteristics in predicting responses to hospitalization for tuberculosis. *Journal of Consulting Psychology*, 19, 65–70.

MORIARTY, J. D. (1954) Evaluation of carbon dioxide inhalation therapy. *American Journal of Psychiatry*, **110**, 765–769.

MORRIS, W. W. (1947) A preliminary evaluation of the Minnesota Multiphasic Personality Inventory. *Journal of Clinical Psychology*, **3**, 370–374.

MOSIER, C. I. (1937) A factor analysis of certain neurotic symptoms. *Psychometrika*, **2**, 263–286.

MURPHY, G. (1922) Types of word-association in dementia praecox, manic-depressives, and normal persons. *American Journal of Psychiatry*, **2**, 539–571.

MURPHY, H. B. M., WITTKOWER, E. D., and CHANCE, N. A. (1967) Crosscultural inquiry into the symptomatology of depression: A preliminary report, *International Journal of Psychiatry*, **3**, 6–15.

MYERS, J. K., and SCHAFFER, L. (1954) Social stratification and psychiatric practice: A study of an out-patient clinic. *American Sociological Review*, **19**, 307–310.

NAMECHE, G. F., WARING, M., and RICKS, D. F. (1964) Early indicators of outcome in schizophrenia. *Journal of Nervous and Mental Disease*, **139**, 232–240.

NAMNUM, A. (1968) The problem of analyzability and the autonomous ego. *International Journal of Psychoanalysis*, **49**, 271–275.

NATHAN, P. E. (1967) *Cues, Decision, and Diagnoses: A Systems-Analytic Approach to the Diagnosis of Psychopathology.* New York: Academic Press.

NATHAN, P. E., ROBERTSON, P., and ANDBERG, M. M. (1969) A system analytic model of diagnosis: IV. The diagnostic validity of abnormal affective behavior. *Journal of Clinical Psychology*, **25**, 235–242.

NATHAN, P. E., SIMPSON, H. F., and ANDBERG, M. M. (1969) A system analytic model of diagnosis: II. The diagnostic validity of abnormal perceptual behavior. *Journal of Clinical Psychology*, **25**, 115–119.

NATHAN, P. E., SAMARAWERRA, A., ANDBERG, M. M., and PATCH, V. D. (1968) Syndromes of psychosis, syndromes of psychoneurosis: A clinical validation study. *Archives of General Psychiatry*, **19**, 704–716.

NATHAN, P. E., ANDBERG, M. M., BEHAN, P. O., and PATCH, V. D. (1969a) Thirty-two observers and one patient: A study of diagnostic validity. *Journal of Clinical Psychology*, **25**, 9–15.

NATHAN, P. E., GOULD, C. F., ZARE, W. C., and ROTH, M. (1969b) A system analytic model of diagnosis: VI. Improved diagnostic validity from median data. *Journal of Clinical Psychology*, **25**, 370–375.

NATHAN, P. E., ROBERTSON, P., ANDBERG, M. M., and PATCH, D. V. (1969c) A system analytic model of diagnosis: III. The diagnostic validity of abnormal cognitive behavior. *Journal of Clinical Psychology*, **25**, 120–130.

NATHAN, P. E., ZARE, N., SIMPSON, H. F., and ANDBERG, M. M. (1969d) A system analytic model of diagnosis: I. The diagnostic validity of psycho-motor behavior. *Journal of Clinical Psychology*, **25**, 3–9.

NEYMANN, C. A., URSE, V. G., MADDEN, J. J., and COUNTRYMAN, M. A. (1943) Electric shock therapy in the treatment of schizophrenia, manic depressive psychoses and chronic alcoholism. *Journal of Nervous and Mental Disease*, **98**, 618–637.

NIELSEN, J. C., GESHELL, S. W., and COEN, R. A. (1942) Review of pharmacologic shock therapy (insulin, picrotoxin and metrazol) at Hastings State Hospital. *Diseases of the Nervous System*, **3**, 122–126.

NIVER, E. O., WEISS, S., and HARRIS, T. H. (1939) Insulin–hypoglycemia treatment of schizophrenia. *American Journal of Psychiatry*, **5**, 799–807.

NOBLE, D. (1951) Hysterical manifestations in schizophrenic illness. *Psychiatry*, **14**, 153–160.

NORTHROP, F. S. C. (1948) *The Logic of the Sciences and the Humanities.* New York: Macmillan.

NOSHPITZ, J. D., and SPEILMAN, P. (1961) Diagnosis study of the differential characteristics of hyperaggressive children. *American Journal of Orthopsychiatry*, **31**, 111–122.

NOTKIN, J., NILES, C. E., DENATALE, F. J., and WITTMAN, G. (1939) A comparative study of hypoglycemic shock treatment and control observations in schizophrenia. *American Journal of Psychiatry*, **96**, 681–688.

NOTKIN, J., DENATALE, F. J., NILES, C. E., and WITTMAN, G. (1940) Comparative study of metrazol treatment and control observations of schizophrenia. *Archives of Neurology and Psychiatry*, **44**, 568–577.

NUTTALL, R. L., and SOLOMON, L. F. (1965) Factorial structure and prognostic significance of premorbid adjustment in schizophrenia. *Journal of Consulting Psychology*, **29**, 362–372.

NUTTALL, R. L., and SOLOMON, L. F. (1970) Prognosis in schizophrenia: The role of premorbid, social class, and demographic factors. *Behavioral Science*, **15**, 255–264.

O'CONNOR, J. P. (1953) A statistical test of psychoneurotic syndromes. *Journal of Abnormal and Social Psychology*, **48**, 581–584.

O'CONNOR, J. P., and STEFIC, E. C. (1959) Some patterns of hypochondriasis. *Educational and Psychological Measurement*, **19**, 363–371.

O'CONNOR, J., STEFIC, E., and GRESOCK, C. (1957) Some patterns of depression. *Journal of Clinical Psychology*, **13**, 122–125.

OLCH, D. R. (1948) Psychometric pattern of schizophrenics on the Wechsler–Bellevue intelligence test. *Journal of Consulting Psychology*, **12**, 127–136.

O'MALLEY, M. (1914) Psychoses in the colored race. *Journal of Insanity*, **71**, 309–336.

OPLER, M. K. (1955) Cultural perspectives in mental health research. *American Journal of Orthopsychiatry*, **25**, 51–59.

OPLER, M. K. (1959) (Ed.), *Culture and Mental Health: Cross Cultural Studies.* New York: Macmillan.

OPLER, M. K. (1963) The need for new diagnostic categories in psychiatry. *Journal of the National Medical Association*, **55**, 133–137.

OPLER, M. K. (1967) *Culture and Social Psychiatry.* New York: Atherton Press.

OPLER, M. K., and SINGER, J. L. (1956a) Ethnic differences in behavior and psychopathology. *International Journal of Social Psychiatry*, **2**, 11–23.

OPLER, M. K., and SINGER, J. L. (1956b) Contrasting patterns of fantasy and mobility in Irish and Italian schizophrenics. *Journal of Abnormal and Social Psychology*, **53**, 42–47.

ORR, W. F., ANDERSON, R. B., MARTIN, M. P., and PHILPOT, D. F. (1955) Factors influencing discharge of female patients from a state mental hospital. *American Journal of Psychiatry*, **111**, 576–582.

OVERALL, B., and ARONSON, H. (1963) Expectations of psychotherapy in patients of lower socioeconomic class. *American Journal of Orthopsychiatry*, **33**, 421–430.

OVERALL, J. E. (1963a) Dimensions of manifest depression. *Journal of Psychiatric Research*, **1**, 239–245.

OVERALL, J. E. (1963b) A configural analysis of psychiatric diagnostic stereotypes. *Behavioral Science*, **8**, 211–219.

OVERALL, J. E., and GORHAM, D. R. (1963) The brief psychiatric rating scale. *Psychological Reports*, **10**, 799–812.

OVERALL, J. E., and HOLLISTER, L. E. (1964) Computer procedures for psychiatric classification. *Journal of the American Medical Association*, **187**, 583–588.

OVERALL, J. E., and HOLLISTER, L. E. (1965) Studies of quantitative approaches to psychiatric classification. In M. M. Katz, J. O. Cole, and W. E. Barton (Eds.), *The Role and Methodology of Classification in Psychiatry and Psychopathology*, pp. 277–299. Washington, D.C.: U.S. Government Printing Office.

OVERALL, J. E., HOLLISTER, L. E., JOHNSON, M., and PENNINGTON, V. (1966) Nosology of depression and differential response to drugs. *Journal of the American Medical Association*, **195**, 946–948.

PACELLA, B. L., and BARRERA, S. E. (1943) Follow-up study of a series of patients treated by electrically induced convulsions and by metrazol convulsions. *American Journal of Psychiatry*, **99**, 513–518.

PAGE, J., LANDIS, C., and KATZ, S. E. (1934) Schizophrenic traits in the functional psychoses and in normal individuals. *American Journal of Psychiatry*, **13**, 1213–1225.

PALMER, D. M., RIEPENHOFF, J. P., and HANAHAN, P. W. (1950) Insulin shock therapy, a statistical survey of 383 cases. *American Journal of Psychiatry*, **106**, 918–926.

PARKES, C. M. (1965a) Bereavement and mental illness: Part 1. A clinical study of the grief of bereaved psychiatric patients. *British Journal of Medical Psychology*, **38**, 1–12.

PARKES, C. M. (1965b) Bereavement and mental illness: II. A classification of bereavement reactions. *British Journal of Medical Psychology*, **38**, 13–26.

PARKIN, A. (1966a) Neuroses and schizophrenia: Historical review. *Psychiatric Quarterly*, **40**, 203–216.

PARKIN, A. (1966b) Neurosis and schizophrenia: II. Modern perspectives. *Psychiatric Quarterly*, **40**, 217–235.

PARLOFF, M. B. (1956) Some factors affecting the quality of therapeutic relationships. *Journal of Abnormal and Social Psychology*, **52**, 5–10.

PASAMANICK, B., DINITZ, S., and LIFTON, L. (1959) Psychiatric orientation in relation to diagnosis and treatment. *American Journal of Psychiatry*, **116**, 127–132.

PASCAL, G. R., SWENSEN, C. H., FELDMAN, D. A., COLE, M. E., and BAYARD, J. (1953) Prognostic criteria in the case histories of hospitalized mental patients. *Journal of Consulting Psychology*, **17**, 163–171.

PATTERSON, C. H. (1948) Is psychotherapy dependent upon diagnosis? *American Psychologist*, **3**, 155–159.

PAYNE, R. W. (1961) Cognitive abnormalities. In H. J. Eysenck (Ed.), *Handbook of Abnormal Psychology*, pp. 193–261. New York: Basic Books.

PEARCE, J., and NEWTON, S. (1963) *The Conditions of Human Growth*. New York: The Citadel Press.

PEPINSKY, H. B. (1948) Diagnostic categories in clinical counseling. *Applied Psychology Monographs*, **15**, 11–13.

PETERS, H. N. (1947) Traits related to improved adjustment of psychotics after lobotomy. *Journal of Abnormal and Social Psychology*, **42**, 383–392.

PETZEL, T. P., and CYNTHER, M. D. (1969) A comparison of psychiatric diagnosis and behavioral classification as criteria for differentiating psychiatric patients. *Journal of General Psychology*, **80**, 219–227.

PHILLIPS, L. (1953) Case history data and prognosis in schizophrenia. *Nervous and Mental Disease*, **117**, 515–525.

PHILLIPS, L. and RABINOVITCH, M. S. (1958) Social role and patterns of symptomatic behavior. *Journal of Abnormal and Social Psychology*, **57**, 181–186.

PHILLIPS, L., and ZIGLER, E. (1964) Role orientation, the action-thought dimension, and outcome in psychiatric disorder. *Journal of Abnormal and Social Psychology*, **68**, 381–389.

PHILLIPS, L., BROVERMAN, I. K., and ZIGLER, E. (1966) Social competence and psychiatric diagnosis. *Journal of Abnormal Psychology*, **71**, 209–214.

PHILLIPS, L., BROVERMAN, I. K., and ZIGLER, E. (1968) Sphere dominance, role orientation, and diagnosis. *Journal of Abnormal Psychology*, **73**, 306–312.

PIOTROWSKI, Z. A. (1945) Experimental psychological diagnosis of mild forms of schizophrenia. *Rorschach Research Exchange*, **9**, 189–200.

PIOTROWSKI, Z. A., and LEWIS, N. D. C. (1950) An experimental Rorschach diagnostic aid for some forms of schizophrenia. *American Journal of Psychiatry*, **107**, 360–366.

PLANT, J. S. (1922) Rating scheme for conduct. *American Journal of Psychiatry*, **1**, 547–572.

PLUTCHIK, R., PLATMAN, S. R., TILLES, R., and FIEVE, R. R. (1970) Construction and evaluation of a test for measuring mania and depression. *Journal of Clinical Psychology*, **26**, 499–503.

POKORNY, A. D. (1960) Characteristics of forty-four patients who subsequently committed suicide. *Archives of General Psychiatry*, **2**, 314–323.

POKORNY, A. D. (1962) Background factors in schizophrenia. *Journal of Nervous and Mental Disease*, **134**, 84–87.

POKORNY, A. D. (1964) Suicide rates in various psychiatric disorders. *Journal of Nervous and Mental Disease*, **139**, 499–506.

POKORNY, A. D., and OVERALL, J. E. (1970) Relationships of psychopathology to age, sex, ethnicity, education and marital status in state hospital patients. *Journal of Psychiatric Research*, **7**, 143–152.

POLATIN, P., and SPOTNITZ, H. (1943) Ambulatory insulin shock technique in the treatment of schizophrenia: An evaluation of therapeutic effects. *Journal of Nervous and Mental Disease*, **97**, 567–575.

POLLOCK, H. M. (1939) A statistical study of 1140 dementia praecox patients treated with metrazol. *Psychiatric Quarterly*, **13**, 558–568.

POWERS, W. T., and HAMLIN, R. M. (1955) Relationship between diagnostic category and deviant verbalization on the Rorschach. *Journal of Consulting Psychology*, **19**, 120–125.

PRATT, S., and TOOLEY, J. (1970) Toward a metataxonomy of human systems actualization: The perspective of contract psychology. In A. R. Mahrer (Ed.), *New Approaches to Personality Classification*, pp. 349–379. New York: Columbia University Press.

PUGH, L. A., and RAY, T. S. (1965) Behavior style categories of chronic schizophrenic women. *Archives of General Psychiatry*, **13**, 457–463.

PUMROY, S. S., and KOGAN, W. S. (1955) The reliability of Wittenborn's scales for rating currently discernible psychopathology. *Journal of Clinical Psychology*, **11**, 411–412.

QUERY, J. M. N., and QUERY, W. T. (1964) Prognosis and progress: A five-year study of forty-eight schizophrenic men. *Journal of Consulting Psychology*, **28**, 501–505.

RABIN, A. I. (1941) Test score patterns in schizophrenia and nonpsychotic states. *Journal of Psychology*, **12**, 91–100.

RABIN, A. I. (1942) Differentiating psychometric patterns in schizophrenia and manic depressive psychosis. *Journal of Abnormal and Social Psychology*, **37**, 270–272.

RABIN, A. I. (1944a) Fluctuations in the mental level of schizophrenic patients. *Psychiatric Quarterly*, **18**, 78–91.

RABIN, A. I. (1944b) Test constancy and variation in the mentally ill. *Journal of General Psychology*, **31**, 231–239.

RACKOW, L., NAPOLI, P. J., KLEBANOFF, S. G., and SCHILLINGER, A. A. (1953) A group method for the rapid screening of chronic psychiatric patients. *American Journal of Psychiatry*, **109**, 561–566.

RAINES, G. N., and ROHRER, J. H. (1955) The operational matrix of psychiatric practice. I. Consistency and variability in interview impressions of different psychiatrists. *American Journal of Psychiatry*, **111**, 721–723.

RAINES, G. N., and ROHRER, J. H. (1960) The operational matrix of psychiatric practice. II. Variability in psychiatric impression and the projection hypothesis. *American Journal of Psychiatry*, **117**, 133–139.

RAMZY, I., and PICKARD, P. M. (1949) A study in the reliability of scoring the Rorschach ink blot test. *Journal of General Psychology*, **40**, 3–10.

RANGELL, L. (1959) The nature of conversion. *Journal of the American Psychoanalytic Association*, **7**, 632–662.

RANSOM, J. A., and GUNDERSON, E. K. E. (1966) Stability in psychiatric diagnosis from hospital admission to discharge. *Journal of Clinical Psychology*, **22**, 140–144.

RAO, C. R., and SLATER, P. (1949) Multivariate analysis applied to differences between neurotic groups. *British Journal of Psychology, Satistical Section*, **2**, 17–29.

RAPAPORT, D., GILL, M., and SCHAFER, R. (1945) *Diagnostic Psychological Testing*. Chicago: Year Book Publications.

RASKIN, A., and GOLOB, R. (1966) Occurrence of sex and social class differences in premorbid competence, symptom and outcome measures in acute schizophrenics. *Psychological Reports*, **18**, 11–22.

RASKIN, A., SCHULTERBRANDT, J. G., and REATIG, N. (1966) Rater and patient characteristics associated with rater differences in psychiatric scale ratings. *Journal of Clinical Psychology*, **22**, 417–423.

RASKIN, A., SCHULTERBRANDT, J., REATIG, N., and RICE, C. E. (1967) Factors of psychopathology in interview, ward behavior and self-report ratings of hospitalized depressives. *Journal of Consulting Psychology*, **31**, 270–278.

READ, C. F., STEINBERG, L., LIEBERT, E., and FINKELMAN, I. (1939) Use of metrazol in the functional psychoses. *American Journal of Psychiatry*, **95**, 781–786.

REDLICH, F. C., HOLLINGSHEAD, A. B., ROBERTS, B. H., ROBINSON, H. A., FREEDMAN, L. Z., and MYERS, J. K. (1953) Social structure and psychiatric disorders. *American Journal of Psychiatry*, **109**, 729–734.

REITZELL, J. M. (1949) A comparative study of hysterics, homosexual and alcoholics using content analysis of Rorschach responses. *Rorschach Research Exchange*, **13**, 127–141.

RENNIE, T. A. C. (1942) Prognosis in manic-depressive psychoses. *American Journal of Psychiatry*, **98**, 801–814.

RENNIE, T. A. C. (1943) Prognosis in manic-depressive and schizophrenic conditions following shock treatment. *Psychiatric Quarterly*, **17**, 642–654.

RENNIE, T. A. C. (1953) Prognosis in the psychoneuroses: Benign and malignant development. In P. Hoch and J. Zubin (Eds.), *Current Problems in Psychiatric Diagnosis*, pp. 66–79. New York: Grune & Stratton.

REZNIKOFF, L. (1940) Evaluation of metrazol shock in treatment of schizophrenia. *Archives of Neurology and Psychiatry*, **43**, 318–325.

REZNIKOFF, L. (1943) Electro shock; indication and results. *Psychiatric Quarterly*, **17**, 355–363.

RICKELS, K., DOWNING, R. W., and DOWNING, M. H. (1966) Personality differences between somatically and psychologically oriented neurotic patients. *Journal of Nervous and Mental Disease*, **142**, 10–18.

RICKERS-OVSIANKANA, M. (1938) The Rorschach test as applied to normal and schizophrenic subjects. *British Journal of Psychology, Medical Section*, **17**, 227–257.

RIEMAN, G. W. (1953) The effectiveness of Rorschach elements in the discrimination between neurotic and ambulatory schizophrenic subjects. *Journal of Consulting Psychology*, **17**, 25–31.

RIVERS, T. D., and BOND, E. D. (1941) Follow-up results in insulin shock therapy after one to three years. *American Journal of Psychiatry*, **98**, 382–384.

ROBERTS, B. H., and MYERS, J. K. (1954) Region, national origin, immigration, and mental disorders. *American Journal of Psychiatry*, **110**, 759–764.

ROBERTSON, R. J., and MALCHICK, D. L. (1968) The reliability of global rating versus specific ratings. *Journal of Clinical Psychology*, **24**, 256–258.

ROBINSON, H. A., REDLICH, F. C., and MYERS, J. K. (1954) Social structure and psychiatric treatment. *American Journal of Orthopsychiatry*, **24**, 307–316.

ROGERS, C. R. (1946) Psychometric tests and client-centered counseling. *Educational and Psychological Measurement*, **6**, 139–144.

ROGERS, C. R. (1971) The concept of the fully functioning person. In A. R. Mahrer and L. Parsons (Eds.), *Creative Developments in Psychotherapy*, pp. 57–73. Cleveland: Case Western Reserve University Press.

ROGERS, L. S. (1951) Differences between neurotics and schizophrenics on the Wechsler–Bellevue Scale. *Journal of Consulting Psychology*, **15**, 151–153.

ROMANO, J., and EBAUGH, F. G. (1938) Prognosis in schizophrenia: A preliminary report. *American Journal of Psychiatry*, **95**, 583–594.

ROSANOFF, A. J. (1920) A theory of personality based mainly on psychiatric experience. *Psychological Bulletin*, **17**, 281–299.

ROSE, J. T. (1963) Reactive and endogenous depression: Response to ECT. *British Journal of Psychiatry*, **109**, 213–217.

ROSEN, A. (1958) Differentiation of diagnostic groups by individual MMPI scales. *Journal of Consulting Psychology*, **22**, 453–457.

ROSEN, A. (1962) Development of the MMPI Scales based on a reference group of psychiatric patients. *Psychological Monographs*, **76**, 1–25.

ROSEN, B., KLEIN, D. F., and GITTLEMAN-KLEIN, R. (1971) The prediction of rehospitalization: The relationship between age of first psychiatric treatment contact, marital status and premorbid social adjustment. *Journal of Nervous and Mental Disease*, **152**, 17–22.

ROSEN, B., KLEIN, D. F., LEVENSTEIN, S., and SHAHINIAN, S. P. (1968) Social competence and posthospital outcome. *Archives of General Psychiatry*, **19**, 165–170.

ROSEN, B., KLEIN, D. F., LEVENSTEIN, S., and SHAHINIAN, S. P. (1969) Social competence and posthospital outcome among schizophrenic and nonschizophrenic psychiatric patients. *Journal of Abnormal Psychology*, **74**, 401–404.

ROSENTHAL, D., and FRANK, J. D. (1958) Fate of psychiatric clinic outpatients assigned to psychotherapy. *Journal of Nervous and Mental Diesease*, **127**, 330–343.

ROSENTHAL, S. H., and GUDEMAN, J. E. (1967) The endogenous depressive pattern: An empirical investigation. *Archives of General Psychiatry*, **16**, 241–249.

ROSENTHAL, S. H., and KLERMAN, G. L. (1966) Content and consistency in the endogenous depressive pattern. *British Journal of Psychiatry*, **112**, 471–484.

ROSENZWEIG, N., VANDENBERG, S. G., MOORE, K., and DUKAY, A. (1961) A study of the reliability of the mental status examination. *American Journal of Psychiatry*, **117**, 1102–1108.

ROSENZWEIG, S. (1934) Types of reaction to frustration: An heuristic classification. *Journal of Abnormal and Social Psychology*, **29**, 298–300.

ROSENZWEIG, S. (1949) Levels of behavior in psychodiagnosis with special reference to the picture-frustration study. *American Journal of Orthopsychiatry*, **20**, 63–72.

ROSS, J. R., and MALZBERG, B. (1939) A review of the results of the pharmacological shock therapy and the metrazol convulsive therapy in New York State. *American Journal of Psychiatry*, **96**, 297–316.

ROSS, J. R., ROSSMAN, I. M., CLINE, W. B., SCHWOERER, O. J., and MALZBERG, B. (1941) The pharmacological shock treatment of schizophrenia: A two-year follow-up study from the New York State hospitals with some recommendations for the future. *American Journal of Psychiatry*, **97**, 1007–1023.

ROTH, M. (1960) Depressive states and their borderlands: Classification, diagnosis and treatment. *Comprehensive Psychiatry*, **1**, 135–155.

ROTTER, J. B. (1967) A new scale for the measurement of interpersonal trust. *Journal of Personality*, **35**, 651–665.

RUBIN, H. (1948) The Minnesota Multiphasic Personality Inventory as a diagnostic aid in a veterans hospital. *Journal of Consulting Psychology*, **12**, 251–254.

RUBIN, M., and SHONTZ, F. C. (1960) Diagnostic prototypes and diagnostic processes of clinical psychologists. *Journal of Consulting Psychology*, **24**, 234–239.

RUBINSTEIN, E. A., and LORR, M. (1956) Comparison of terminators and remainers in outpatient treatment. *Journal of Clinical Psychology*, **12**, 345–349.

RUPP, C., and FLETCHER, E. K. (1940) A five to ten year follow-up study of 641 schizophrenic cases. *American Journal of Psychiatry*, **96**, 877–888.

SABOT, L. M., PECK, R., and RASKIN, J. (1969) The waiting room society: A study of families and children applying to a child psychiatric clinic. *Archives of General Psychiatry*, **21**, 25–32.

SACHSON, A. D., RAPPOPORT, L., and SINNETT, E. R. (1970) The Activity Record: A measure of social isolation-involvement. *Psychological Reports*, **26**, 413–414.

SACKS, J. M., and LEWIN, R. S. (1950) Limitations of the Rorschach as sole diagnostic instrument. *Journal of Consulting Psychology*, **14**, 479–481.

SALZMAN, L. (1947) An evaluation of shock therapy. *American Journal of Psychiatry*, **103**, 669–679.

SANDIFER, M. G., PETTUS, C., and QUADE, D. (1964) A study of psychiatric diagnosis. *Journal of Nervous and Mental Disease*, **139**, 350–356.

SANDIFER, M. G., WILSON, I. C., and GREEN, L. (1966) The two type thesis of depressive disorders. *American Journal of Psychiatry*, **123**, 93–97.

SANDLER, J., and HAZARI, A. (1960) The "obsessional": On the psychological classification of obsessional character traits and symptoms. *British Journal of Medical Psychology*, **33**, 113–122.

SARBIN, T. R. (1944) The logic of prediction in psychology. *Psychological Review*, **51**, 210–228.

SCHAFFER, L., and MYERS, J. K. (1954) Psychotherapy and social stratification: An empirical study of practice in a psychiatric outpatient clinic. *Psychiatry*, **17**, 83–93.

SCHEIER, I. H., and CATTELL, R. B. (1958) Confirmation of objective test factors and assessment of their relation to questionnaire factors: A factor analysis of 113 rating, questionnaire and objective test measurements of personality. *Journal of Mental Science*, **104**, 608–624.

SCHILDER, P. (1934) Experiments on after-images, imagination and hallucinations. *American Journal of Psychiatry*, **13**, 597–611.

SCHMIDT, H. O. (1945) Test profiles as a diagnostic aid: The Minnesota Multiphasic Inventory. *Journal of Applied Psychology*, **29**, 115–131.

SCHMIDT, H. O., and FONDA, C. P. (1956) The reliability of psychiatric diagnosis: A new look. *Journal of Abnormal and Social Psychology*, **52**, 262–267.

SCHOFIELD, W., HATHAWAY, S. R., HASTINGS, D. W., and BELL, D. M. (1954) Prognostic factors in schizophrenia. *Journal of Consulting Psychology*, **18**, 155–166.

SCHWAB, J. J., BIALOW, M. R., BROWN, J. M., HOLZER, C. E., and STEVENSON, B. E. (1967) Sociocultural aspects of depression in medical inpatients. II. Symptomatology and class. *Archives of General Psychiatry*, **17**, 539–543.

SCHWARTZ, M. D., and ERRERA, P. (1963) Psychiatric care in a general hospital emergency room. *Archives of General Psychiatry*, **9**, 113–121.

SEITZ, F. C. (1970) Five psychological measures of neurotic depression: A correlational study. *Journal of Clinical Psychology*, **26**, 504–505.

SHADER, R. I., KELLAM, S. G., and DURELL, J. (1967) Social field events during the first week of hospitalization as predictors of treatment outcome for psychotic patients. *Journal of Nervous and Mental Disease*, **145**, 142–153.

SHAKOW, D. (1965) The role of classification in the development of the science of psychopathology with particular reference to research. In M. M. Katz, J. O. Cole, and W. E. Barton (Eds.), *The Role and Methodology of Classification in Psychiatry and Psychopathology*, pp. 116–143. Washington, D.C.: U.S. Government Printing Office.

SHAKOW, D. (1966) The role of classification in the development of the science of psychopathology with particular reference to research. *Bulletin of the Menninger Clinic*, **30**, 150–160.

SHARMA, S. L. (1970) A historical background of the development of nosology in psychiatry and psychology. *American Psychologist*, **25**, 248–253.

SHERMAN, I. C., and KRAINES, S. H. (1943) Environmental and personality factors in the psychoses. *Journal of Nervous and Mental Disease*, **97**, 676–691.

SIEGEL, N. H., KAHN, R. L., POLLACK, M., and FINK, M. (1963) Social class, diagnosis, and treatment in three psychiatric hospitals. *Social Problems*, **62**, 191–196.

SIEGEL, S. M. (1956) The relationship of hostility to authoritarianism. *Journal of Abnormal and Social Psychology*, **52**, 368–372.

SILVER, R. J., and SINES, L. K. (1961) MMPI characteristics of a state hospital population. *Journal of Clinical Psychology*, **17**, 142–146.

SILVERMAN, D. (1941) Prognosis in schizophrenia: A study of 271 cases. *Psychiatric Quarterly*, **15**, 477–493.

SIMMONS, W. L., and TYLER, F. B. (1969) Length of hospitalization as a function of patients' conceptions of therapists. *Journal of Clinical Psychology*, **25**, 332–338.

SIMON, R. J., FISHER, B., FLEISS, J. L., GURLAND, B. J., and SHARPE, L. (1971) Relationship between psychopathology and British- or American-oriented diagnosis. *Journal of Abnormal Psychology*, **78**, 26–29.

SIMON, W., and WIRT, R. D. (1961) Prognostic factors in schizophrenia. *American Journal of Psychiatry*, **117**, 887–890.

SINES, L. K., and SILVER, R. J. (1963) An index of psychopathology (Ip) derived from clinical judgments of MMPI profiles. *Journal of Clinical Psychology*, **19**, 324–326.

SLATER, E. (1961) The thirty-fifth Maudsley Lecture: "Hysteria 311." *Journal of Mental Science*, **107**, 359–381.

SLAVSON, S. R. (1950) *Analytic Group Psychotherapy*. New York: Columbia University Press.

SMITH, J. A. (1952) An evaluation of the results of treatment of 33 patients with carbon dioxide inhalation. *American Journal of Psychiatry*, **109**, 626.

SMITH, L. H., HASTINGS, D. W., and HUGHES, J. (1943) Immediate and follow up results of electroshock therapy. *American Journal of Psychiatry*, **100**, 351–354.

SMITH, L. H., HUGHES, J., HASTINGS, D. W., and ALPERS, B. J. (1942) Electroshock treatment in the psychoses. *American Journal of Psychiatry*, **98**, 558–561.

SMITH, W. G. (1966) A model for psychiatric diagnosis. *Archives of General Psychiatry*, **14**, 521–529.

SNYGG, D., and COMBS, A. W. (1949) *Individual Behavior*. New York: Harper.

SOMOPOULOS, V. (1971) Hysterical psychosis: Psychopathological aspects. *British Journal of Medical Psychology*, **44**, 95–100.

SPEARMAN, C. E. (1929) The Tenth Maudsley Lecture: The psychiatric use of the methods and results of experimental psychology. *Journal of Mental Science*, **75**, 357–370.

SPITZER, R. L., and ENDICOTT, J. (1968) Diagno: A computer program for psychiatric diagnosis utilizing the Differential Diagnostic Procedure. *Archives of General Psychiatry*, **18**, 746–756.

SPITZER, R. L., and WILSON, P. T. (1968) A guide to the American Psychiatric Association's new diagnostic nomenclature. *American Journal of Psychiatry*, **124**, 1619–1629.

SPITZER, R. L., COHEN, J., FLEISS, J. L., and ENDICOTT, J. (1967) Quantification of agreement in psychiatric diagnosis: A new approach. *Archives of General Psychiatry*, **17**, 83–87.

SPITZER, R. L., ENDICOTT, J., FLEISS, J. L., and COHEN, J. (1970) The psychiatric status schedule: A technique for evaluating psychopathology and impairment in role functioning. *Archives of General Psychiatry*, **23**, 41–55.

SPITZER, R. L., FLEISS, J. L., BURDOCK, E. I., and HARDESTY, A. (1964) The mental status schedule: Rationale, reliability, and validity. *Comprehensive Psychiatry*, **6**, 384–395.

SPITZER, R. L., FLEISS, J., KERNOHAN, W., LEE, J. C., and BALDWIN, I. T. (1965) Mental Status Schedule: Comparing Kentucky and New York schizophrenics. *Archives of General Psychiatry*, **12**, 448–455.

STAGNER, R. (1948) *Psychology of Personality*. New York: McGraw-Hill.

STAINBROOK, E. (1953) Some historical determinants of contemporary diagnostic and etiological thinking in psychiatry. In P. H. Hoch and J. Zubin (Eds.), *Current Problems in Psychiatric Diagnosis*, pp. 3–18. New York: Grune & Stratton.

STAINBROOK, E. (1954) A cross-cultural evaluation of depressive reactions. In P. H. Hoch and J. Zubin (Eds.), *Depression*, pp. 39–50. New York: Grune & Stratton.

STEEN, R. R. (1933) Prognosis in manic-depressive psychoses with a report of factors studied in 493 patients. *Psychiatric Quarterly*, **7**, 419–424.

STENBACK, A., and ACHTE, K. A. (1966) Hospital first admissions and social class. *Acta Psychiatrica*, **42**, 113–124.

STEPHENS, J. H., and ASTRUP, C. (1963) Prognosis in "process" and "non-process" schizophrenia. *American Journal of Psychiatry*, **119**, 945–953.

STEPHENS, J. H., ASTRUP, C., and MANGRUM, J. C. (1966) Prognostic factors in recovered and deteriorated schizophrenics. *American Journal of Psychiatry*, **122**, 1116–1121.

STEPHENS, J. H., ASTRUP, C., and MANGRUM, J. C. (1967) Prognosis in schizophrenia. *Archives of General Psychiatry*, **16**, 693–698.

STEPHENS, J. H., O'CONNOR, G., and WIENER, G. (1969) Long-term prognosis in schizophrenia using the Becker–Wittman Scale and the Phillips Scale. *American Journal of Psychiatry*, **126**, 498–504.

STEPHENSON, W. (1931) Studies in experimental psychiatry: I. A case of general inertia. *Journal of Mental Science*, **77**, 723–741.

STEPHENSON, W. (1932a) Studies in experimental psychiatry: II. Some contact of p-factor with psychiatry. *Journal of Mental Science*, **78**, 315–330.

STEPHENSON, W. (1932b) Studies in experimental psychiatry: III. p-score and inhibition for high-p praecox cases. *Journal of Mental Science*, **78**, 908–928.

STEVENS, S. S. (1936) Psychology: The propaedeutic science. *Philosophy of Science*, **3**, 90–103.

STOLLER, R. J., and GEERTSMA, R. H. (1963) The consistency of psychiatrists' judgments. *Journal of Nervous and Mental Disease*, **137**, 58–66.

STONE, L. A. (1969) Psychiatrists' judgmental evaluation of susceptibility to external stress for selected disorder classification stimuli. *Journal of Clinical Psychology*, **25**, 21–26.

STONE, L. A., and SKURDAL, M. A. (1968) Judged prognosis for functional psychosis disorder classification: A prosthetic continuum. *Journal of Consulting and Clinical Psychology*, **32**, 469–472.

STORROW, H. (1962) Psychiatric treatment and the lower-class neurotic patient. *Archives of General Psychiatry*, **6**, 469–473.

STOTSKY, B. A., and LAWRENCE, J. F. (1955) Various Rorschach indices as discriminators of marked and little conceptual disorganization among schizophrenics. *Journal of Consulting Psychology*, **19**, 189–193.

STRECKER, H. P. (1938) Insulin treatment of schizophrenia. *Journal of Mental Science*, **84**, 146–155.

STRUPP, H. H. (1958a) The performance of psychiatrists and psychologists in a therapeutic interview. *Journal of Clinical Psychology*, **14**, 219–226.

STRUPP, H. H. (1958b) The psychotherapists' contribution to the treatment process. *Behavioral Science*, **3**, 34–67.

STRUPP, H., and WILLIAMS, J. (1960) Some determinants of clinical evaluation of different psychiatrists. *Archives of General Psychiatry*, **2**, 434–440.

STUDMAN, L. G. (1935) Studies in experimental psychiatry: V. "W" and "f" factors in relation to traits of personality. *Journal of Mental Science*, **81**, 107–137.

SULLIVAN, P. L., MILLER, C., and SMELSER, W. (1958) Factors in length of stay and progress in psychotherapy. *Journal of Consulting Psychology*, **22**, 1–9.

SWENSEN, C. H. (1957) Empirical evaluations of human figure drawings. *Psychological Bulletin*, **54**, 431–466.

SWENSEN, C. H. (1968) Empirical evaluations of human figure drawings: 1957–1966. *Psychological Bulletin*, **70**, 20–44.

SWENSEN, C. H., and PASCAL, G. R. (1954a) Prognostic significance of type of onset of mental illness. *Journal of Consulting Psychology*, **18**, 127–130.

SWENSEN, C. H., and PASCAL, G. R. (1954b) Duration of illness as a prognostic indicator in mental illness. *Journal of Consulting Psychology*, **18**, 363–365.

SZASZ, T. S. (1956) Some observations on the relationship between psychiatry and the law. *Archives of Neurology and Psychiatry*, **75**, 297–315.

SZASZ, T. S. (1957) Some observations on the use of tranquilizing drugs. *Archives of Neurology and Psychiatry*, **77**, 86–92.

SZASZ, T. S. (1959) The classification of "mental illness." *Psychiatric Quarterly*, **33**, 77–101.

SZASZ, T. S. (1961a) The uses of naming and the origin of the myth of mental illness. *American Psychologist*, **16**, 59–65.

SZASZ, T. S. (1961b) *The Myth of Mental Illness*. New York: Harper & Row.

SZASZ, T. S. (1966) The psychiatric classification of behavior: A strategy of personal constraint. In L. D. Eron (Ed.), *The Classification of Behavior Disorders*, pp. 123–170. Chicago: Aldine.

TAMKIN, A. (1959) An MMPI scale measuring severity of psychopathology. *Journal of Clinical Psychology*, **15**, 56.

TATOM, M. H. (1958) A factorial isolation of psychiatric outpatient syndromes. *Journal of Consulting Psychology*, **22**, 73–81.

TATOM, M. H. (1961) Psychiatric outpatient personality patterns. *Journal of Consulting Psychology*, **25**, 275.

TAULBEE, E. S., and SISSON, B. D. (1957) Configurational analysis of MMPI profiles of psychiatric groups. *Journal of Consulting Psychology*, **21**, 413–417.

TAULBEE, E. S., SISSON, B. D., and GASTON, C. O. (1956) Affective ratio and 8-9-10 per cent on the Rorschach test for normals and psychiatric groups. *Journal of Consulting Psychology*, **20**, 105–108.

TAYLOR, J. A. (1953) A personality scale of manifest anxiety. *Journal of Abnormal and Social Psychology*, **48**, 285–290.

TAYLOR, J. A., and VON SALZEN, C. F. (1938) Prognosis in dementia praecox, *Psychiatric Quarterly*, **12**, 576–582.

TEMERLIN, M. K. (1968) Suggestion effects in psychiatric diagnosis. *Journal of Nervous and Mental Disease*, **147**, 349–353.

TEMKIN, O. (1965) The history of classification in the medical sciences. In M. M. Katz, J. O. Cole, and W. E. Barton (Eds.), *The Role and Methodology of Classification in Psychiatry and Psychopathology*, pp. 11–20. Washington, D.C.: U.S. Government Printing Office.

TEMOCHE, A., PUGH, T. F., and MACMAHON, B. (1964) Suicide rate among current and former mental institution patients. *Journal of Nervous and Mental Disease,* **138,** 124–130.

THIESEN, J. W. (1952) A pattern analysis of structural characteristics of the Rorschach test in schizophrenia. *Journal of Consulting Psychology,* **16,** 365–370.

THORNE, F. C. (1945) Directive psychotherapy: IV. The therapeutic implications of the case history. *Journal of Clinical Psychology,* **1,** 318–330.

THORNE, F. C. (1949) The attitudinal pathoses. *Journal of Clinical Psychology,* **5,** 1–21.

THORNE, F. C. (1953) The frustration–anger–hostility states: A new diagnostic classification. *Journal of Clinical Psychology,* **9,** 334–339.

THORNE, F. C. (1964) Diagnostic classification and nomenclature for psychological states. *Journal of Clinical Psychology,* **20,** 3–60.

THORNE, F. C. (1967) *Integrative Psychology.* Brandon, Vermont: Clinical Psychology Publishing Company.

THORNE, F. C. (1970a) Diagnostic implications of integrative psychology. In A. R. Mahrer (Ed.), *New Approaches to Personality Classification,* pp. 311–345. New York: Columbia University Press.

THORNE, F. C. (1970b) Diagnostic classification and nomenclature for existential state reactions. *Journal of Clinical Psychology, Monograph Supplement,* No. 30.

THORNE, F. C., and NATHAN, P. E. (1969) The general validity of official diagnostic classifications. *Journal of Clinical Psychology,* **25,** 375–383.

THORNE, F. C., and NATHAN, P. E. (1970) Systems analysis methods for integrative diagnosis. *Journal of Clinical Psychology,* **26,** 3–17.

THURRELL, R. J., and LEVITT, H. (1967) Psychiatric agreement regarding patient "attractiveness." *Comprehensive Psychiatry,* **8,** 189–197.

THURSTONE, L. L. (1934) The vectors of the mind. *Psychological Review,* **41,** 1–32.

THURSTONE, L. L., and THURSTONE, T. G. (1930) A neurotic inventory. *Journal of Social Psychology,* **1,** 3–30.

TIETZE, C., LEMKAU, P., and COOPER, M. (1941) Schizophrenia, manic-depressive psychosis, and social-economic status. *American Journal of Sociology,* **47,** 167–175.

TREHUB, A., and SCHERER, I. W. (1958) Wechsler–Bellevue scatter as an index of schizophrenia. *Journal of Consulting Psychology,* **22,** 147–149.

TROUTON, D. S., and MAXWELL, A. E. (1956) The relation between neurosis and psychosis: An analysis of symptoms and past history of 819 psychotics and neurotics. *Journal of Mental Science,* **102,** 1–21.

TURNER, R. J. (1968) Class and mobility in schizophrenic outcome. *Psychiatric Quarterly,* **42,** 712–725.

ULLMAN, L. P., and GUREL, L. (1962) Validity of symptom rating from psychiatric records. *Archives of General Psychiatry,* **7,** 130–134.

VAILLANT, G. E. (1962) The prediction of recovery in schizophrenia. *Journal of Nervous and Mental Disease,* **135,** 534–543.

VAILLANT, G. E. (1963) The natural history of the remitting schizophrenias. *American Journal of Psychiatry,* **120,** 367–376.

VAILLANT, G. E. (1964) Prospective prediction of schizophrenic remissions. *Archives of General Psychiatry,* **11,** 509–518.

VARVEL, W. A. (1941) The Rorschach test in psychotic and neurotic depression. *Bulletin of the Menninger Clinic*, **5**, 5–12.

VERNIS, J. S. (1968) Interview and the Bernreuter Personality Inventory for screening adjustment problems in college students. *Psychological Reports*, **23**, 49–50.

VESTRE, N. D. (1966) Validity data on the Psychotic Reaction Profile. *Journal of Consulting Psychology*, **30**, 84–85.

VESTRE, N. D., and ZIMMERMAN, R. (1970) Validation study of the Psychotic Inpatient Profile. *Psychological Reports*, **27**, 3–7.

VIETH, I. (1957) Psychiatric nosology: From Hippocrates to Kraeplin. *American Journal of Psychiatry*, **114**, 385–391.

VINSON, D. B. (1960) Responses to the Rorschach test that identify schizophrenic thinking, feeling, and behavior. *Journal of Clinical and Experimental Psychopathology*, **21**, 34–40.

VON BERTALANFFY, L. (1951) Theoretical models of biology and psychology. *Journal of Personality*, **20**, 24–38.

WALKER, R. G., and KELLEY, F. E. (1960) Predicting the outcome of a schizophrenic episode. *Archives of General Psychiatry*, **2**, 492–503.

WALLACH, M. S. (1962) Therapists' patient preferences and their relationship to two patient variables. *Journal of Clinical Psychology*, **18**, 497–501.

WALLACH, M. S., and STRUPP, H. H. (1960) Psychotherapists' clinical judgments and attitudes towards patients. *Journal of Consulting Psychology*, **24**, 316–323.

WANKLIN, J. M., FLEMING, D. F., BUCK, C. W., and HOBBS, G. E. (1956) Discharge and readmission among mental hospital patients: Cohort analysis. *Archives of Neurology and Psychiatry*, **76**, 660–669.

WARD, C. H., BECK, A. T., MENDELSON, M., MOCK, J. E., and ERBAUGH, J. K. (1962) The psychiatric nomenclature. *Archives of General Psychiatry*, **7**, 198–205.

WARNER, S. J. (1950) The Wechsler–Bellevue psychometric pattern in anxiety neurosis. *Journal of Consulting Psychology*, **14**, 297–304.

WATKINS, J. G., and STAUFFACHER, J. C. (1952) An index of pathological thinking in the Rorschach. *Journal of Projective Techniques*, **16**, 276–286.

WATSON, C. G. (1965a) WAIS profile patterns of hospitalized brain-damaged and schizophrenic patients. *Journal of Clinical Psychology*, **21**, 294–296.

WATSON, C. G. (1965b) Intratest scatter in hospitalized brain-damaged and schizophrenic patients. *Journal of Consulting Psychology*, **29**, 596.

WATSON, C. G., and LOGUE, P. E. (1968) A note on the interjudge reliability of Phillips and Elgin Scale ratings. *Journal of Clinical Psychology*, **24**, 64–66.

WATSON, R. I. (1949) Diagnosis as an aspect of the clinical method: A review. In *Readings in the Clinical Method in Psychology*, pp. 405–427. New York: Harper & Brothers.

WATSON, R. I. (1951a) The function of diagnosis. In *The Clinical Method in Psychology*, pp. 21–36. New York: Harper & Brothers.

WATSON, R. I. (1951b) *The Clinical Method in Psychology*. New York: Harper & Brothers.

WECHSLER, D. (1944) *The Measurement of Adult Intelligence*. 3rd ed. Baltimore: Williams & Wilkins.

WECHSLER, H., GROSSER, G. H., and BUSFIELD, B. L. (1963) The depression rating scale. *Archives of General Psychiatry*, **9**, 334–343.

WECKOWICZ, T. E., MUIR, W., and CROPLEY, A. J. (1967) A factor analysis of the Beck Inventory of Depression. *Journal of Consulting Psychology*, **31**, 23–28.

WEIDER, A. (1943) Effects of age on the Bellevue intelligence scales in schizophrenic patients. *Psychiatric Quarterly*, **17**, 337–346.

WEIL, A. P. (1953) Clinical data and dynamic considerations in certain cases of childhood schizophrenia. *American Journal of Orthopsychiatry*, **23**, 518–529.

WEINER, I. B. (1961) Three Rorschach scores indicative of schizophrenia. *Journal of Consulting Psychology*, **25**, 436–439.

WEINER, I. B. (1962) Rorschach tempo as a schizophrenic indicator. *Perceptual and Motor Skills*, **15**, 139–141.

WEINER, I. B. (1964) Pure C and color stress as Rorschach indicators of schizophrenia. *Perceptual and Motor Skills*, **18**, 484.

WEINER, I. B. (1965) Follow-up validation of Rorschach tempo and color use indicators of schizophrenia. *Journal of Projective Techniques and Personality Assessment*, **29**, 387–391.

WEINSTOCK, H. I. (1965) The role of classification in psychoanalytic practice. In M. M. Katz, J. O. Cole, and W. E. Barton (Eds.), *The Role and Methodology of Classification in Psychiatry and Psychopathology*, pp. 62–72. Washington, D.C.: U.S. Government Printing Office.

WEISMAN, A. D. (1965) *The Existential Core of Psychoanalysis*. Boston: Little, Brown & Company.

WELLS, F. L. (1913) Experimental pathology of the higher mental processes. *Psychological Bulletin*, **10**, 213–224.

WELLS, F. L. (1914) Experimental psychopathology. *Psychological Bulletin*, **11**, 202–212.

WERTHEIMER, M. (1953) On the supposed behavioral correlates of an "eye" content response on the Rorschach. *Journal of Consulting Psychology*, **17**, 189–194.

WHEELER, W. M., LITTLE, K. B., and LEHNER, G. F. J. (1951) The internal structure of the MMPI. *Journal of Consulting Psychology*, **15**, 134–141.

WHITEHEAD, D. (1937) Prognosis in dementia praecox. *Psychiatric Quarterly*, **11**, 383–390.

WHITEHEAD, D. (1938) Improvement and recovery rates in dementia praecox without insulin therapy. *Psychiatric Quarterly*, **12**, 405–413.

WILLIAMS, G. H., WILLIAMS, G. H., JR., KINGSBURY, H. M., and BIXBY, D. E. (1939) Experience with the pharmacological shock treatment of schizophrenia. *American Journal of Psychiatry*, **95**, 811–813.

WILLIAMS, H. V., LIPMAN, R. S., UHLENHUTH, E. H., RICKELS, K., COVI, L., and MOCK, J. (1967) Some factors in influencing the treatment expectations of anxious neurotic outpatients. *Journal of Nervous and Mental Disease*, **145**, 208–220.

WILLIAMS, H. V., LIPMAN, R. S., RICKELS, K., COVI, L., UHLENHUTH, E. H., and MATTSON, N. B. (1968) Replication of symptom distress factors in anxious neurotic outpatients. *Multivariate Behavioral Research*, **3**, 199–212.

WILLIAMS, R. R., and POTTER, H. W. (1921) The significance of certain symptoms in the prognosis of dementia praecox. *State Hospital Quarterly*, **6**, 361–380.

WILSON, D. C. (1939) The results of shock therapy in the treatment of affective disorders. *American Journal of Psychiatry*, **96**, 673–679.

WILSON, M. S., and MEYER, E. (1962) Diagnostic consistency in a psychiatric liaison service. *American Journal of Psychiatry*, **119**, 207–209.

WINDER, A. E., and HERSKO, M. (1955) Effect of social class on length and type of treatment in a Veterans Administration Mental Hygiene clinic. *Journal of Clinical Psychology*, **11**, 77–79.

WING, J. K. (1961) A simple reliable subclassification of chronic schizophrenia. *Journal of Mental Science*, **107**, 862–875.

WINNE, J. F. (1951) A scale of neuroticism: An adaptation of the Minnesota Multiphasic Personality Inventory. *Journal of Clinical Psychology*, **7**, 117–122.

WINNICOTT, D. W. (1965) Classification: Is there a psycho-analytic contribution to psychiatric classification? In *The Maturational Process and the Facilitating Environment*, pp. 124–139. New York: International Universities Press.

WISDOM, J. O. (1961) A methodological approach to the problem of hysteria. *International Journal of Psychoanalysis*, **42**, 224–237.

WITTENBORN, J. R. (1949) An evaluation of the use of Bellevue–Wechsler subtest scores as an aid in psychiatric diagnosis. *Journal of Consulting Psychology*, **13**, 433–439.

WITTENBORN, J. R. (1950a) Symptom patterns in a group of mental hospital patients. *Journal of Consulting Psychology*, **14**, 290–302.

WITTENBORN, J. R. (1950b) A new procedure for evaluating mental hospital patients. *Journal of Consulting Psychology*, **14**, 500–501.

WITTENBORN, J. R. (1951) Symptom patterns in a group of mental hospital patients. *Journal of Consulting Psychology*, **15**, 290–302.

WITTENBORN, J. R. (1962) The dimensions of psychosis. *Journal of Nervous and Mental Disease*, **134**, 117–128.

WITTENBORN, J. R. (1963) Distinctions within psychotic dimensions. *Journal of Nervous and Mental Disease*, **137**, 541–547.

WITTENBORN, J. R. (1964) Psychotic dimensions in male and female hospitalized patients: Principal component analysis. *Journal of Nervous and Mental Disease*, **138**, 460–467.

WITTENBORN, J. R., and BAILEY, C. (1952) The symptoms of involutional psychosis. *Journal of Consulting Psychology*, **16**, 13–17.

WITTENBORN, J. R., and HOLZBERG, J. D. (1951a) The generality of psychiatric syndromes. *Journal of Consulting Psychology*, **15**, 372–380.

WITTENBORN, J. R., and HOLZBERG, J. D. (1951b) The Wechsler–Bellevue and descriptive diagnosis. *Journal of Consulting Psychology*, **15**, 325–329.

WITTENBORN, J. R., and LESSER, G. S. (1951) Biographical factors and psychiatric symptoms. *Journal of Clinical Psychology*, **7**, 317–322.

WITTENBORN, J. R., and SMITH, J. B. K. (1964) A comparison of psychotic dimensions in male and female hospitalized patients. *Journal of Nervous and Mental Disease*, **138**, 375–382.

WITTENBORN, J. R., and WEISS, W. (1952) Patients' diagnosed manic-depressive psychosis-manic state. *Journal of Consulting Psychology*, **16**, 193–198.

WITTENBORN, J. R., HOLZBERG, J. D., and SIMON, B. (1953) Symptom correlates for descriptive diagnosis. *Genetic Psychological Monographs*, **47**, 237–301.

WITTENBORN, J. R., MANDLER, G., and WATERHOUSE, I. K. (1951) Symptom patterns in youthful mental hospital patients. *Journal of Clinical Psychology*, **7**, 323–327.

WITTENBORN, J. R., PLANTE, M., and BURGESS, F. (1961) A comparison of physicians' and nurses' symptom ratings. *Journal of Nervous and Mental Disease*, **133**, 514–518.

WITTMAN, P. (1941) A scale for measuring prognosis in schizophrenic patients. *Elgin State Hospital Papers*, **4**, 20–33.

WITTMAN, P. (1944) Follow-up on Elgin prognosis scale results. *Illinois Psychiatric Journal*, **4**, 56–59.

WITTMAN, P. (1948) Diagnostic and prognostic significance of the shut-in personality type as a prodromal factor in schizophrenia. *Journal of Clinical Psychology*, **4**, 211–214.

WITTMAN, P., and SHELDON, W. (1948) A proposed classification of psychotic behavior reactions. *American Journal of Psychiatry*, **105**, 124–128.

WITTMAN, P., and STEINBERG, D. L. (1944) A study of prodromal factors in mental illness with special reference to schizophrenia. *American Journal of Psychiatry*, **100**, 811–816.

WOLSTEIN, B. (1964) *Transference: Its Structure and Function in Psychoanalytic Therapy*. New York: Grune & Stratton.

YAMAMOTO, J., and GOIN, M. K. (1966) Social class factors relevant for psychiatric treatment. *Journal of Nervous and Mental Disease*, **142**, 332–339.

YAMAMOTO, J., JAMES, Q. C., BLOOMBAUM, M., and HATTEM, J. (1967) Racial factors in patient selection. *American Journal of Psychiatry*, **124**, 630–638.

YOUNG, R. J. (1950) The Rorschach diagnosis and interpretation of involutional melancholia. *American Journal of Psychiatry*, **106**, 748–749.

ZEIFERT, M. (1941) Results obtained from the administration of 12,000 doses of metrazol to mental patients. *Psychiatric Quarterly*, **15**, 772–778.

ZETZEL, E. R. (1968) The so-called good hysteric. *International Journal of Psychoanalysis*, **49**, 256–260.

ZIEGLER, F. J., and IMBODEN, J. B. (1962) Contemporary conversion reactions. *Archives of General Psychiatry*, **6**, 279–287.

ZIGLER, E., and PHILLIPS, L. (1960) Social effectiveness and symptomatic behaviors. *Journal of Abnormal and Social Psychology*, **61**, 231–238.

ZIGLER, E., and PHILLIPS, L. (1961a) Psychiatric diagnosis and symptomatology. *Journal of Abnormal and Social Psychology*, **63**, 69–75.

ZIGLER, E., and PHILLIPS, L. (1961b) Social competence and outcome in psychiatric disorder. *Journal of Abnormal and Social Psychology*, **63**, 264–271.

ZIGLER, E., and PHILLIPS, L. (1961c) Psychiatric diagnosis: A critique. *Journal of Abnormal and Social Psychology*, **63**, 607–618.

ZIGLER, E., and PHILLIPS, L. (1962) Social competence and the process-reactive distinction in psychopathology. *Journal of Abnormal and Social Psychology*, **65**, 215–222.

ZILBOORG, G. (1954) The changing concept of man in present-day psychiatry. *American Journal of Psychiatry*, **111**, 445–448.

ZILBOORG, G., and HENRY, G. W. (1941) *A History of Medical Psychology*. New York: Norton.

ZISKIND, E., SOMERFELD-ZISKIND, E., and ZISKIND, L. (1942) Metrazol therapy in the affective psychoses: Study of a controlled series of cases. *Journal of Nervous and Mental Disease*, **95**, 460–473.

ZUBIN, J. (1965) Biometric assessment of mental patients. In M. M. Katz, J. O. Cole, and W. E. Barton (Eds.), *The Role and Methodology of Classification in Psychiatry and Psychopathology*, pp. 353–373. Washington, D.C.: U.S. Government Printing Office.

AUTHOR INDEX

Page references in *italic type* are to the reference list at the end of the book

127

136 AUTHOR INDEX

Schulterbrandt, J. G.   36, 39, 67, *114*
Schwab, J. J.   69, *117*
Schwartz, M. D.   69, *117*
Schwartz, M. L.   32, 65, *98*
Schwoerer, O. J.   58, 62, *116*
Scrivner, J.   71, *102*
Seidenberg, B.   76, *99*
Seitz, F. C.   79, *117*
Selesnick, S.   2, *83*
Sells, S. B.   68, *90*
Shader, R. I.   61, *117*
Shahinian, S. P.   61, *115*, *116*
Shakow, D.   5, 71, *117*
Sharma, S. L.   73, *117*
Sharpe, L.   68, 71, *96*, *101*, *118*
Sheldon, W.   11, 13, *125*
Sherman, I. C.   22, *117*
Sherman, L.   58, 59, 61, 62, *104*
Sherman, L. J.   58, 61, *107*
Shontz, F. C.   71, *116*
Siegel, N. H.   68, *100*, *117*
Siegel, S. M.   79, *117*
Silver, R. J.   11, 29, 52, 78, *117*, *118*
Silverman, D.   58, 59, 61, *118*
Silverman, S.   58, 61, 62, *88*
Simmons, W. L.   59, *118*
Simon, B.   35, *124*
Simon, R.   59, *91*
Simon, R. J.   68, *118*
Simon, W.   59, 61, *118*
Simpson, H. F.   10, *110*
Sines, L. K.   11, 29, 52, 78, *117*, *118*
Singer, J. L.   68, 69, *111*
Sinnett, E. R.   8, 9, *116*
Sisson, B. D.   29, 31, *120*
Skurdal, M. A.   8, 57, 71, *119*
Slater, E.   55, 66, 76, *99*, *118*
Slater, P.   42, 76, *99*, *114*
Slavson, S. R.   60, *118*
Smelser, W.   70, *120*
Smith, J. A.   58, 62, *118*
Smith, J. B. K.   11, 16, 69, *124*
Smith, L. H.   58, *118*
Smith, P. A.   8, *85*
Smith, R. S.   58, 61, *104*
Smith, W. G.   71, *118*
Snygg, D.   60, *118*
Solomon, L. F.   59, 61, *111*
Somerfeld-Ziskind, E.   58, 62, *125*

Somopoulos, V.   55, *118*
Sonenthal, I. R.   58, 59, 61, 62, *105*
Sonn, T. M.   36, 39, *105*
Spearman, C. E.   12, 67, 74, *118*
Spielman, P.   75, *111*
Spitzer, R. L.   5, 8, 67, 68, 71, *118*
Spotnitz, H.   58, 62, *113*
Sprague, J.   67, *85*
Stafford, J. W.   9, 10, 11, 18, 24, 36, *105*
Stagner, R.   1, *118*
Stainbrook, E.   2, 69, 76, *119*
Stauffacher, J.   8, 61, 78, 79, *99*, *106*, *122*
Steen, R. R.   59, 61, *119*
Stefic, E. C.   54, *110*
Steinberg, D. L.   28, 62, *125*
Steinberg, L.   58, 62, *114*
Stenback, A.   69, *119*
Stephens, J. H.   59, 61, *119*
Stephenson, W.   76, *119*
Stevens, S. S.   76, *119*
Stevenson, B. E.   69, *117*
Stiel, A.   39, 40, *102*
Stilson, D. W.   71, *94*
Stoker, D.   69, *107*
Stoller, R. J.   67, 71, *110*
Stone, A. R.   70, *93*, *99*
Stone, C. D.   *91*
Stone, G. B.   *104*
Stone, L. A.   8, 57, 58, 71, 79, *119*
Storrow, H.   70, *119*
Stotsky, B. A.   12, 31, *119*
Strecker, H. P.   58, 59, 61, 62, *119*
Strupp, H. H.   70, 71, *119*, *120*, *122*
Studman, L. G.   76, *120*
Stumpf, J. C.   25, *88*
Sugerman, A. A.   61, *87*
Sullivan, P. L.   70, *120*
Sundland, D. M.   61, *94*
Swartz, J. D.   69, *91*
Swensen, C. H.   58, 61, 71, *88*, *92*, *112*, *120*
Swerdloff, B.   76, 78, *100*
Szasz, T. S.   68, 72, 74, 75, 76, *120*

Taffel, C.   75, *90*
Tainter, Z. C.   63, *83*
Tamkin, A.   78, *120*

SUBJECT INDEX